# Stede Bonnet

## Charleston's Gentleman Pirate

### Christopher Byrd Downey

Charleston | London

THE
History
PRESS

Published by The History Press
Charleston, SC 29403
www.historypress.net

First published 2012

Manufactured in the United States

ISBN 978.1.60949.540.4

Library of Congress CIP data applied for.

*For Lizzie Porcher White.*

Better far to live and die
Under the brave black flag I fly,
Than play a sanctimonious part,
With a pirate head and a pirate heart.

—*Pirates of Penzance, Gilbert and Sullivan*

# Contents

# Foreword and Acknowledgements

Ifirst read about Stede Bonnet, the "gentleman pirate," while a senior in high school in Robert E. Lee's *Blackbeard the Pirate: A Reappraisal of His Life and Times*. In Lee's book, Stede Bonnet is, as he is in just about every other book on the topic, a comic footnote to the Golden Age of Piracy. The story of the silly gentleman who left his life of wealth and luxury and decided to play pirate—but instead played the fool. Most writers on the subject of piracy have really only used the short chapter on Stede Bonnet in Captain Charles Johnson's *A General History of Pirates*, written in 1719, as the basis for telling the unflattering story of the Barbadian planter-turned-pirate. Just like any other reader of Lee's book, I scoffed at the ridiculousness of Bonnet's story and lost myself in the adventure and legend of the infamous Blackbeard.

In my senior year of high school in Colonial Heights, Virginia, my real passion was not long dead pirates—it was baseball. Skinny and awkward, I was basically talentless, but somehow I imagined myself as a lights-out, hard-throwing pitcher with an untouchable fastball and a curveball that could buckle the knees of even the most hardened batter. I was sure that, with some practice and the right coaching, I could play college baseball and maybe even play at a professional level. However, halfway through my senior season, much to my surprise, I had not yet gotten my first win of the season as we faced off in a home game against our neighboring rivals from Petersburg. Petersburg was without a doubt the worst team in our district, and I looked forward to notching my first overdue win.

Late into the fifth inning, I was hanging on to a three-run lead and had managed to load the bases with two outs. Petersburg's first baseman, who was as skinny and as awkward looking as me, strode to the plate. I felt a sense of relief at the prospect of the easy out at the plate being the veritable last nail in Petersburg's late rally. My first pitch was a curveball that hung over the plate like a fat Italian meatball. The batter's eyes opened wide, and I swear I saw a grin. A pitcher does not need to see the ball traveling over his head to know it has been hit well. He can tell when a homerun has been hit by the sound of the bat striking the ball. I hung my head as the batter trotted leisurely around first base. Suddenly a thunderous, gong-like sound came from right field and settled over the stadium. Confused, I turned towards the right field wall and quickly located the source. Standing directly behind the right field wall, a huge water tank that serviced the southern end of Colonial Heights rested on steel legs seventy feet above the ground. The ball had been hit so hard that it not only had left the park but also had firmly struck the towering water tank. No one in the stadium that day had ever seen a baseball hit that hard.

I didn't even wait for my coach to come to the mound to pull me out of the game. Walking past my disappointed coach as I made my way to the dugout, I could see people in the stands laughing and pointing at the water tank. The entire Petersburg team was still surrounding its hero at home plate, celebrating the monstrous grand slam. I was humiliated. My baseball dreams were over with that one swing of the bat. I couldn't even beat the worst team in our district, and I would forever be a footnote in that first baseman's story of the day he hit a ball so far that it struck the top of a water tower. Ostracized to the end of the bench, the strangest thought came into my mind. I thought of Stede Bonnet. Surely, just like me that day in the dugout, Stede had his own moment of clarity when he realized that sometimes you just aren't the person that you necessarily hope and imagine yourself to be. Life isn't fair. Sometimes the best you can do is just to try. Deep in the grips of my own personal pity party, I thought of the antihero pirate and concluded that if I had been a pirate nearly three hundred years ago, my story probably would have turned out the same as Stede Bonnet. I thought to myself, "Someone should tell Stede Bonnet's story." Twenty years later, I have finally gotten around to doing just that.

Perusing the aisle of the history section of bookstores, I now have a newfound respect for authors. It can be a lonely world, spending countless hours in front of a computer or rifling through stacks of historical records trying to recreate the past. Looming deadlines and the strain of the writing process can take a toll on a writer. I would like to thank a few of those people who helped ease the strain and contributed to the creation of this book. A special thank you to Mike Coker at the Old Exchange Building and Allan Stello at the Powder Magazine, both in Charleston, for their guidance and assistance. I owe a great debt of gratitude to Gianpaolo Porcu and Jennifer Capps for their help with the pictures in the book. I would like to thank Elise Detterbeck for opening to me her beautiful home, Trott's Cottage. Thank you to Bill McIntosh and Dr. William Rhett from St. Phillip's Church in Charleston. I appreciate the assistance of the lovely ladies at the North Carolina Maritime Museum at Southport, North Carolina. Also thanks for the kindness and cooperation of the staff of the South Carolina Historical Society, the Charleston Library Society and the Charleston Public Library Main Branch. Thank you to my family for their support.

Unless otherwise noted, all images appear courtesy of the author's collection.

## *I*

# Nassau

September, 1717—The sloop made the turn into Nassau Harbor and fell off the wind under the protection of Hog Island. A growing crowd of pirates on the beach watched the new arrival, anxious as to whether this vessel was friend or foe. As the sloop edged closer, the pirates could see the newcomer flew the pirate's Jolly Roger from her mast. The onlookers drew a collective sigh of relief as they watched the sloop's black flag snapping in the wind.

The newcomer's handling of the sails seemed awkward and lubberly to the seasoned pirates in Nassau that day. But a closer examination of the sloop revealed why—these pirates had recently been engaged in a deadly battle. Her hull and railing were pockmarked from shot. Her sails and rigging were tattered. The crew on deck was only half that which would be necessary to handle a vessel of her size. Their faces looked anxious and drawn. Beneath their bare feet, the deck was splintered and blood-stained. The shattered panes of glass of the captain's great cabin on the stern were a telltale sign that this sloop's opponent had not just tried to escape these pirates but had also sought to destroy them by maneuvering behind, raking the sloop with cannon fire from stern to bow. Predator had become prey.

The sparse crew dropped the anchor, breaking the harbor's clear, pristine water. Nassau harbor was littered with dozens of merchant vessels of various nationalities. Most were stripped of masts, riggings and fittings. Some were half submerged, with exposed timbers still smoldering from having been set on fire before sinking. The harbor was a veritable junkyard of prizes taken by the pirates of the island.

Three fathoms below the newly arrived sloop, her anchor gripped the harbor bottom, and she swung tightly and securely on the anchor line. Another pirate had found refuge in Nassau.

The crew lowered her longboat into the water. Several of the pirates manned the oars and sheepishly propelled the boat toward the beach. Even the longboat had been damaged in the sloop's recent action, and one of the pirates bailed buckets of water over the side as they made their way toward the crowded beach. The onlookers waded into the water and blocked the longboat from landing. The exhausted pirates were overwhelmed by the barrage of questions: "Who are you? Where did you come from? What had happened to your vessel?" Fearful, the newcomers did their best to answer the questions. They explained that they were the pirate vessel *Revenge* from Barbados and had been "on the account" for about six months. A couple days prior to their arrival in Nassau, they had engaged a Spanish warship and had nearly been destroyed. Half of her original crew of seventy was dead or below deck, recovering from wounds. It was only through the speed advantage of their sloop over the much larger Spanish ship that the pirates were able to avoid annihilation. The pirates who had survived the battle unscathed were exhausted from standing nonstop watches for the last two days as they made their way to Nassau.

"Why would a ten-gun sloop engage a Spanish man-of-war?" asked one of the crowd. "We were ordered to by our captain," came the response. "What kind of fool captain gave that order?" another bystander demanded. "Captain Stede Bonnet," was the terse answer. Two of the pirates on the beach, who were from Barbados, shot a curious glance at one another, and then one asked, "You don't mean Major Stede Bonnet of Barbados?" "Aye, that be him," growled the pirate still bailing water from the bottom of the longboat.

As the group looked back towards the sloop riding at anchor, a figure emerged from the captain's great cabin and came onto the deck. Wearing a silken dressing gown and his head wrapped in bandages, the figure limped to the rail and stared at the Nassau waterfront. He looked pale and frightened, and in his hand was a leather-bound book. Now allowed to drag their longboat onto the beach, one of the pirates pointed back at the figure on the deck and said in a mocking tone, "Look, there be our Captain Bonnet now."

Across the harbor, on the deck of his own sloop, another pirate was watching the events unfolding in Nassau that day with keen interest. A privateer-turned-pirate, he had learned the pirate trade as first mate to

Benjamin Hornigold, but now he commanded his own pirate ship. His name was Edward Thatch, but the world would come to know him as Blackbeard. He saw something in the pitiful figure of this Stede Bonnet from Barbados that no one else in Nassau saw that day. He saw *opportunity*.

Nassau in the early eighteenth century was a pirate's utopia. Located on the island of New Providence in the Bahamas, Nassau was named in honor of King William II from the Dutch house of Orange-Nassau, who would later become King William III of England. The Bahamas consisted of over seven hundred islands, but by start of the eighteenth century, New Providence was one of only a few populated islands, with Nassau as its only real town.

When Sir Nicholas Trott arrived as governor in 1694, there were less than one hundred full-time residents in Nassau. He built a fort overlooking Nassau harbor, but the island's small population did not allow for proper manning of the defenses. Repeated raids by the French and the Spanish had thwarted any population growth as residents would flee, mostly to the safety of Jamaica. Those who did remain on the fledgling colony suffered under a repressed economy that required the importation of almost all goods and wares. Consequently, the island residents were not averse to buying the relatively cheap smuggled goods from the occasional visiting pirate. The series of governors sent by the Lord Proprietors to the island starting in 1670 were also, in many cases, complicit with the pirates. Governor Nicholas Trott was no exception. When Henry Avery and his crew of one hundred other pirates arrived in Nassau harbor in 1696 on board the forty-six-gun ship *Fancy*, her holds filled with treasure, Avery openly bribed Trott to allow him and his fellow pirates to come ashore and dispose of their ill gotten goods. However, human frailty aside, there would be two major events that would form the perfect storm and seal Nassau's reputation as a pirate's nest and the centerpiece in what history would come to refer to as the "Golden Age of Piracy." Roughly encompassing the first quarter of the eighteenth century, the Golden Age of Piracy would be a period when as many as five thousand men would go "on the account"—living and, many times, dying as pirates in the waters of the Americas and the Caribbean.

Edmund Dummer, who developed the first mail service between England and the islands of the Caribbean, wrote in 1702, "it is the opinion of everyone that this cursed trade [privateering] will breed so many pirates that when peace comes, we shall be in more danger from them than we are now from the enemy." The "peace" that Dummer was referring to was the end of the War of Spanish Succession. Upon the death of King Charles II of Spain in 1700, the European superpowers settled in to a war that spread to the Caribbean and the Americas. Deformed in mind and body, King Charles II of Spain was the product of generations of inbreeding among Spain's ruling Hapsburg family in an effort to maintain the royal bloodline. Described as "short, lame, epileptic, senile…and always on the verge of death," Charles demanded at one point that his deceased family members be exhumed so that he could look upon their corpses. Not surprisingly, when Charles died at thirty-nine years of age, he was childless. In his last will, Charles named Philip, Duke of Anjou and grandson of King Louis XIV of France, as the heir to the Spanish throne. The consolidation of the throne of France and Spain was an unacceptable proposition to England

King Charles II of Spain.

and her allies, namely the Dutch and the Austrians. A near-global war erupted. The portion of the war fought in the Americas and the Caribbean came to be called Queen Anne's War, in honor of the reigning monarch of England. A fairly unremarkable tenure as Queen, her reign was punctuated in 1707 by the Act of Union, which unified the thrones of England and Scotland, creating the Kingdom of Great Britain.

Unable to raise and outfit a navy on a scale large enough to fight a war as vast as this war was to become, Britain, as well as every other nation involved, turned to the practice of privateering. A privateer was, in essence, a legalized pirate. Private individuals and ships during wartime could apply for and receive from the government a Letter of Marque.

This Letter of Marque authorized the private party to attack and plunder vessels of enemy nations. The issued documents were very explicit as to which nation's vessels could be attacked and the percentage of plunder that would be due to the government. The draw for sailors was, of course, not a sense of patriotism but the promise of prize money. Thousands of sailors from North American ports joined the ranks of privateering vessels. The risk of death in battle was outweighed by dreams of prize money from capturing enemy vessels. Prize money from the capture of just one enemy vessel could be more than a year's pay serving in the Royal Navy.

Queen Anne.

An uneasy peace came in 1713 with the signing of the Treaty of Utrecht. Philip was recognized as the King of Spain, but he renounced any claim of succession to the throne of France. Throughout the Caribbean and along the eastern seaboard in cities like Charleston, Williamsburg, Philadelphia, New York and Boston, thousands of sailors who had served for years as privateers found themselves out of work and restless. The leap from privateer to pirate was a short one, but it would take a natural disaster to spark the piracy powder keg.

In July 1715, a Spanish treasure fleet of eleven vessels sailed from Havana bound for Cadiz. Since the start of the war, fearful of the threat of privateers, the Spanish had avoided moving large amounts of gold, silver and other treasures from their colonies in Mexico and the Caribbean to Spain. Subsequently, this particular treasure fleet was heavily laden and departing very late in the season. Less than a week into the voyage, as the convoy sailed along the southeastern coast of Florida, the fleet was decimated by a hurricane. The force of the easterly winds forced the vessels onto the reefs near the shore, tearing the bottom out of ships and throwing sailors into the confused seas. Only one vessel of the fleet was able to escape the wrath of the hurricane. The other ten vessels were destroyed over a forty-mile stretch of reef, and more than a thousand men were killed. As many as another thousand survivors swam and crawled onto the beach. A fortune in Spanish gold and silver bullion had been spread across the bottom of the sea in fairly shallow and clear water. The Spanish survivors immediately began to dive the wrecks and recover lost treasure. A makeshift fort was built on the beach to protect the recovered bullion, and the survivors waited for rescue.

Spanish doubloons from the Spanish treasure fleet wreck of 1715.

News of the treasure fleet's demise and the magnitude of unclaimed treasure resting at the bottom of the ocean spread through the Caribbean and North America like lightning. Unemployed privateers from Jamaica to Boston were quick to fit out vessels and sail to the Florida coast to go "a-wrecking." Henry Jennings, a former privateer, was one of the first to arrive at the wrecks. Not satisfied to just dive the wrecks for treasure, Jennings and his men mounted an attack on the Spanish encampment guarding the treasure that had been recovered. Overwhelmed by the sheer number of pirates, the Spanish surrendered without a shot being fired. Soon, the wrecks were swarming with vessels trying to recover treasure from the ocean bottom. Periodically, the Spanish would send a ship of war to the wrecks and run off the marauders. Nassau was the closest English-speaking port, so the "wreckers" would retreat to its protected harbor. Soon the island's population swelled, and Nassau was the base of operation for those who had answered the call of the Spanish treasure wrecks.

When the wrecks had been fished dry, outright piracy against merchant vessels was the next natural course of action for the growing collection of rogues. Nassau was strategically located adjacent to the busy shipping lanes of the Florida Straits, which was the ocean superhighway facilitating the movement of goods between Europe and the colonies in the Americas and the Caribbean. Initially, the pirates confined their attacks to vessels of nations that were traditional enemies of Great Britain. Veteran pirate captains, like Benjamin Hornigold and Henry Jennings, refused to allow their crews to attack any English vessels, preying only on French and Spanish vessels. However, it was not long before vessels from all nations, including Great Britain, were fair game for the new generation of pirates operating out of Nassau.

As the pirate stronghold grew in Nassau, the Admiralty office in London was being flooded with letters from colonial governors and merchants seeking relief. Virginia's lieutenant governor Alexander Spotswood wrote to London in 1716 of the growing issue of piracy in Nassau, stating it would "prove dangerous to British commerce if not timely suppressed." George Logan, speaker of the House of Assembly in Charleston, wrote a plea regarding the planned departure from Charleston harbor of the Royal Navy warship *Shoreham.*

> *By reason of the design the Pirates of the Bahama Islands (and who are numerous) have to attack…we cannot suppose, that any such persons have a regard to, or make any difference or distinction, between the people of any nation whatsoever: we ought to provide for the safety and defence of the Inhabitants of this Province. This house humbly conceives; that it would be requisite…his Majesty Ship* Shoreham *to stay some time longer here with said Ship and that it would in some measure deter the Pirates from coming here.*

*So the Treasure was Divided* by Howard Pyle. A group of pirates anxiously watch as their plunder is divided on a deserted beach.

The plea fell on deaf ears. In April 1717, the *Shoreham* sailed to Virginia and then back to England. But London was getting word of a bigger threat than just the threat to commerce. The pirates posed a threat to the very fabric of British government.

The Glorious Revolution of 1688 deposed the Catholic King James II of the Stuarts and effectively removed the possibility of a Catholic monarch on the English throne. When Queen Anne died without a direct heir, the difficult question of succession set the newly unified Kingdom of Great Britain at odds with itself and with its neighbors. Many, especially in Scotland and the north of England, supported James III, son of the deposed Catholic King James II and half brother of Queen Anne. (To further confuse

James Francis Edward Stuart (James III). Referred to by his detractors as the "Pretender," his claim to the throne was supported by many of the pirates of the Golden Age of Piracy, including Stede Bonnet and Blackbeard. Supporters of James III were known as Jacobites.

historians, the supporters of James III were called Jacobites.) However, Parliament acted quickly to pass the 1701 Act of Settlement and gave the throne to Anne's very distant relative, George, of the Hanover family, from present-day Germany. King George I could not even speak English when he ascended to the throne, but what was important to his backers was that he was Protestant. The majority of the pirates based in Nassau were from families and regions of Great Britain that were sympathetic to the claim of James III to the throne. Intelligence reached London that the pirates of Nassau were forming a Jacobite armada to invade Great Britain and convey James III (or the "Pretender," as his detractors called him) to the throne. Certainly a far-flung notion, but there was cause for fear as there had been an unsuccessful Jacobite uprising in 1715 that started in Scotland but quickly lost steam. The Jacobites were, if nothing else, persistent, and uprisings would continue for another thirty years with no success. Direct descendants of the Hanoverian King George I still occupy the British throne today.

# 2

# Barbados

Aside from his Jacobite sentiments, Stede Bonnet shared little in common with the other pirates of Nassau. Born to Edward Bonnet and his wife, Sarah, in 1688 on the island of Barbados in the Parish of Christ Church, near the capital of Bridgetown, Stede entered a world of wealth and privilege. His great-grandfather had been one of the first wave of English immigrants to the island in the early seventeenth century. Although tobacco was initially the planned cash crop of the island, the pioneers of the island quickly found sugarcane to be more successful.

Unlike New Providence in the Bahamas, Barbados had an overpopulation problem. By the start of the eighteenth century, Barbados had a population of nearly sixty thousand people. Two-thirds of this population were slaves who worked the sweltering sugarcane fields. The island was also heavily populated by large numbers of indentured servants—individuals who had signed contracts of specific years of servitude in exchange for conveyance to the colony. Considering that Barbados was only twenty-one miles at its widest point and was filled with huge, sprawling plantations, space was certainly at a premium. The island's success with sugarcane had made Barbados the richest and most highly developed of the English colonies. But by the time of Stede's birth, due to the overpopulation and the shortage of available land, people were leaving Barbados in record numbers. Many were coming to the Carolinas, particularly the lowlands around Charleston, to utilize their acquired agricultural skills.

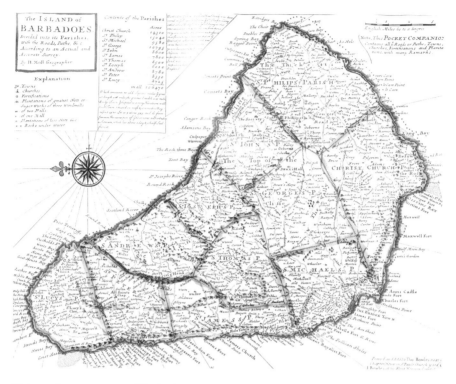

Eighteenth-century map of Barbados.

By the time of the writing of his will in 1676, Stede's grandfather, Thomas Bonnet, had built an estate of 400 acres, which included at least two windmills that were used to grind syrup from the cane. He leased out an additional 120 acres, and he also owned a townhome on High Street in Bridgetown. In his will, Thomas left the majority of his estate to his younger son, Edward, Stede's father. His graciousness to his younger son does not seem to be a slight to his older son, Thomas Jr. Thomas the elder had already settled a substantial estate on his older son that same year on the occasion of his marriage.

Stede had two younger sisters, Frances and Sarah, with whom he enjoyed an aristocratic upbringing. On Sundays, they would worship at St. Michael's Church in Bridgetown, where their father served on the vestry, and during the week, they received a liberal education. The family's needs were attended to by a staff of house servants, and nearly one hundred slaves worked the estate's sugarcane fields. Stede was being groomed to take his place among the next generation of Barbadian gentleman planters.

In June 1695, when Stede was only seven years old, his father died. In his will, Stede's father made ample provisions for the well-being of his family. The importance of a good education was clearly of paramount importance in the Bonnet family, and Edward had even made unconventional arrangements in his will to ensure the education of his two daughters. He also allocated funds to complete the building of the estate's new mansion that was under construction at the time of his death. When Stede's mother died shortly after her husband, a Mr. John Gibbs gained guardianship of Stede and his sisters. However, in July of 1699, when Stede was eleven years old, a petition was brought before the Barbados Council Chamber requesting that guardianship of the Bonnet children be removed from Mr. Gibbs and granted to Jennet Whetstone. Mrs. Whetstone was the widow of Edward Bonnet's old friend John Whetstone, the former Deputy Secretary of Barbados. Records do not indicate why Mrs. Whetstone sought to revoke Mr. Gibbs's guardianship, but one could speculate that perhaps with the death of Stede's father, the newly widowed Sarah Bonnet was a target for those with an eye for the wealth of the Bonnet estates. Mr. Gibbs may

The ruins of an eighteenth-century windmill in Barbados. Windmills were used on the sprawling plantations to grind syrup from sugarcane.

have convinced Sarah to name him executor of the Bonnet estate, which included the children. Upon Sarah's death, the responsibilities involved in caring for three young children were probably not priorities for Mr. Gibbs, and Mrs. Whetstone may have felt compelled to intervene. Whatever the circumstances, Mrs. Whetstone seems to have been an important part of Stede's life until her death in 1708, which coincided with the approximate time that Stede fully inherited his father's estate and took his place among the Barbados aristocracy.

Stede wasted no time in enlarging his wealth and estate. When he was twenty-one years old, Stede began courting sixteen-year-old Mary Allamby. The two were married in 1709 at St. Michaels Church. Mary was the eldest of six daughters of another leading Barbadian planter, Colonel William Allamby, from the neighboring Parish of St. Thomas. Colonel Allamby owned one hundred acres and was the senior member of his parish's General Assembly. He bequeathed further acreage and fortune to Stede upon the marriage to his daughter. In June 1652, a law had been passed in Barbados that bestowed military rankings upon the land-owning aristocracy based on acreage owned. A mere fifty acres of land earned the rank of captain. With the consolidation of his own estate and those lands received from Mary's father on his wedding day, Stede became Major Stede Bonnet. He had not served a day on a drill field or marched at the head of a column of soldiers. He had only read books about the life of a soldier, but he would now be addressed by his peers as "Major." Stede was regarded as "a gentleman of good reputation…master of plentiful fortune and had the advantage of a liberal education" and "he was generally esteemed and honoured." Life was looking pretty good for the young Stede. But all was not well in the Bonnet household.

Stede and Mary welcomed their first child in May 1712: a son, Allamby Bonnet. The couple's joy did not last as Allamby died within his first year—an unfortunate but not uncommon event in an age of soaring infant mortality rates. Stede was devastated. Three more children followed over the next few years—Edward, Stede Jr. and Mary—but Stede was not able to shake the depression he suffered following Allamby's death. By the birth of his last child, Mary, in early 1717, Stede's neighbors and friends described him as suffering "from a disorder in his mind, which had been but too visible in him."

Adding further stress to the Major's fragile psyche was trouble in his marriage. Like many couples that marry at a very young age, the Bonnets argued…a lot. Mary seemed to have had a propensity for nagging. Captain

# Charleston's Gentleman Pirate

Charles Johnson in the 1724 *A General History of Pirates* writes eloquently describing Stede's difficulties with Mary as "occasioned by some discomforts he found in a married state." To escape his "discomforts," Stede would retreat to his well-stocked library and lose himself in his books. By the time Mary was pregnant with their last child, Stede had developed a passion for reading about nautical matters, including ship armaments, navigation and seamanship. Although he did live near Barbados's only port in Bridgetown, Stede had no maritime background and was "ill qualified for the business, as not understanding maritime affairs." He was especially enchanted by the plentiful stories reported in newspapers regarding pirates prowling the Caribbean and their attacks on merchant vessels. The pirate adventures were well documented and very popular reading in the early eighteenth century. The pirate motto of a "short but merry life" set Stede to daydreaming of a life beyond the dull routine of managing his family and estate.

When Stede told Mary that he had put a down payment on the construction of a sloop of war to hunt pirates, she must have shook her head and rolled her eyes. Equivalent to a modern-day middle aged man buying an Italian sports car or a Harley Davidson motorcycle, Stede's friends and family probably attributed his decision to a premature midlife crisis. He explained to Mary and others that he planned to go to Jamaica and obtain a commission from the governor to hunt pirates. He rationalized that the prize money of the capture of a pirate ship would bring fast financial reward. Everyone must have thought Stede's sanity had finally gone over the edge. But Stede was sitting on a secret that was even more shocking: he planned to become a pirate himself.

Each day, Stede would make his way down to the Bridgetown waterfront to check on the progress of his new investment under construction in the shipyard. He was having a sixty-ton Bermuda-style sloop built. This particular design was popular among pirates. Fast and nimble, the Bermuda sloop was also shallow-drafted, which allowed it to sail into coves and inlets not accessible to a larger, more powerful, pursuing vessel. The Bermuda sloop was single-masted with a simple fore-and-aft rigged sail configuration—a large main mast aft and a smaller foresail. Although fairly light, the Bermuda sloop was still commodious enough to carry heavy armaments. Stede's sloop would carry ten cannons. The shipwrights building the sloop did receive one strange request from the owner. The captain's great cabin was to be filled with plenty of shelving—this pirate ship would have a library.

The next part of Stede's transition to pirate would be more difficult than the building of a ship. He would have to locally find an able

A model of an eighteenth-century Bermuda sloop. Stede Bonnet had a sixty-ton sloop of this style built in a Bridgetown shipyard in 1717. *Photo by author.*

crew of seaman willing to turn pirate. Prowling the seedy taverns of the Bridgetown waterfront, Stede in his silken suit and cravat, with a powdered wig on his head, must have drawn long, suspicious looks from the hardened sailors swilling rum. His job was further complicated by the fact that he would have to recruit a pirate crew that would keep his secret until they sailed. For whatever "disorder in his mind" that Stede may have suffered, he proved to have a silver tongue and to be an able salesman because he quickly recruited a crew of seventy men. Ignoring the tradition of pirates and privateers receiving their pay through the shares of plunder, Stede took the unprecedented step of paying his crew a salary. Since he had no practical experience as the captain of a ship, Stede would have to pay his new officers well since he would be almost completely dependent on their skills.

While waiting for his pirate ship to be completed, Stede made sketches of a design for his own pirate flag. The English pirates referred to the various flags of their brethren as the "Death's Head" or the "Jolly Roger."

Earlier French pirates, or buccaneers, had flown a blood-red banner that was called the "Jolie Rouge" or "pretty red." The all-red flag had a tradition in naval combat of being a signal of "no quarter" being offered to an enemy—a veritable guarantee of a fight to the death. The English pirates corrupted the French "Jolie Rouge" into "Jolly Roger." The flags of the Golden Age of Piracy were generally black, with images of skulls or skeletons that represented the deadly nature of the pirate's vocation. Some flags also incorporated images of an hourglass, symbolic of the short life of those who resisted, as well as daggers, spears and bleeding hearts.

By the spring of 1717, the sloop was completed and stocked with provisions, powder, shot and, of course, an ample library of books. Stede christened his new pirate ship *Revenge*. One can only speculate whether it was named for revenge against a nagging wife, a life of tedium or the demons that haunted Stede since Allamby's death. But on a clear May night, without even bidding a farewell to his wife and children, Stede and seventy pirates quietly sailed on the ebbing tide. In an effort to stem the illegal exodus of indentured servants and debtors, the Barbados General Assembly had recently passed a law requiring anyone leaving the island to register with the secretary's office and obtain a ticket. Consequently, as the *Revenge* turned to the northwest and slipped out of Carlisle Bay, Stede was already an outlaw. Major Stede Bonnet would never see his family or Barbados again.

Stede Bonnet's pirate flag. The flags of pirates were collectively referred to as the "Jolly Roger."

Pacing the quarterdeck, the new pirate captain in his wig, knee britches, stockings and polished, buckled shoes stood in stark contrast to his barefoot, salty and sun-worn crew. As the *Revenge* transitioned from the calm, clear waters of the bay into the steady, rolling swells of the open ocean, Stede was suddenly overcome with nausea. Pale and in a cold sweat, he gripped the leeward rail and vomited over the side. The crew on the quarterdeck shot knowing glances at one another. The captain was seasick. Stede's nearly thirty years of a sedentary life on a sugarcane plantation had not lent itself to developing "sea legs." Assisted by a couple of the crew, Stede retreated to his cabin and collapsed in his bunk.

The next morning, a meeting was held in the captain's great cabin to determine the *Revenge*'s course. Stede, still sick in bed, instructed that he wanted to put as many miles as possible between himself and his previous life in Barbados. A course was to be set for the capes off of Virginia, more than two thousand miles away. Furthermore, the captain gave orders that he was no longer to be called "Captain Bonnet." The crew was to address him as "Captain Edwards." Although anxious to leave his previous life behind, Stede's name change was most likely an effort to spare his children any shame in the event of his capture. The *Revenge* skirted the Bahamas and caught the speed-boosting current of the Gulf Stream, arriving off the coast of Virginia in June 1717.

The new pirates were initially very successful. In their first week lurking off the busy trade lanes of the royal colony of Virginia, the crew of the *Revenge* captured four merchant vessels without firing a shot. The pirate's black flag and ten cannons proved motivation enough for their prey to hove to and surrender. The first was the *Anne*, commanded by Captain Montgomery, from Glasgow, Scotland. Her capture was quickly followed by the *Young*, also from Scotland, and then the *Endeavor*, commanded by Captain Scot, of Bristol, England. The three vessels were plundered of their valuables, which included clothes, money and ammunition. But then came the more complicated capture of the *Turbet*. A sensation not unlike the seasickness that had racked Stede for the last few weeks came over him when he read the papers of the *Turbet*'s captain. The *Turbet* was from Bridgetown, Barbados, and the captain and crew were not fooled by the man calling himself "Captain Edwards." They were certainly surprised to see Major Bonnet commanding a pirate sloop. The crew of the *Turbet* was transferred to one of the other prizes, and Stede ordered the Barbadian vessel burned. The *Turbet* would not be returning to Barbados with Stede's secret.

An engraving of Stede Bonnet from Captain Charles Johnson's *A General History of Pirates*.

The *Revenge* then headed north towards New York. Off the northeast end of Long Island, they captured a sloop bound for the Caribbean. Running short of provisions that could not be plundered from their prizes, Stede landed a small group of his crew at Gardiners Island. Still not completely comfortable or familiar with his role as pirate captain, Stede did not give orders to forcibly pillage the coastal residents of Gardiners Island but rather gave the landing party a grocery list and a roll of cash.

Gardiners Island was no stranger to pirates. Nearly two decades earlier, William Kidd had landed at Gardiners Island prior to returning to New York to face charges of piracy. The once-venerable Kidd shared much in common with Bonnet. Once an esteemed citizen of New York, the restless Kidd sought and received a privateer's commission. However, lack of success and the dissent of his crew led to the questionable capture of the *Quedah Merchant* in the Indian Ocean in January 1698. Upon his return to New York, he was arrested and sent to London to stand trial. Professing his innocence, Kidd was abandoned by his original privateering backers and crucial evidence that supported Kidd's defense was conveniently lost. Upon being found guilty and sentenced to hang, Kidd said, "My Lord, it is a very hard sentence. For my part, I am the innocentest person of them all, only I have been sworn against by perjured persons." He tried to use his alleged buried treasure at Gardiners Island as a bargaining tool to avoid the noose, but he was unsuccessful and was hanged in May 1701 at Execution Dock at Wapping in London. Treasure hunters still seek his buried treasure on Gardiners Island today.

Peaceably completing their errand, the pirates, in their longboat loaded with provisions, returned to the *Revenge*. Stede gave the order to weigh anchor and steer a southerly course to the busy port of Charleston, South Carolina. They arrived off the Charleston bar in early August 1717.

Charleston (actually called Charles Town until the American Revolution) was first founded in 1670. Named in honor of King Charles II, Charleston was the capital of the Province of Carolina which originally included both North and South Carolina. Unlike the royal colony of Virginia to the north, the Carolinas were a proprietary colony. When King Charles II regained the throne after the English Civil War, which had culminated in the beheading of his father King Charles I and a near–ten year period in England with no king on the throne, favors were granted by the King upon those who had remained loyal during the royal absence. King Charles II gave eight noblemen (Lord Proprietors) the deed to the vast tract of lands that encompassed the Province of Carolina. By the time of the *Revenge*'s arrival, Charleston was the only city of note in the Carolinas. The earliest settlers had built a trading hub out of a remote, mosquito-infested peninsula at the confluence of the Cooper and Ashley Rivers. (Present-day Charlestonians proudly declare that the Cooper and Ashley combine to form the Atlantic Ocean.) Hundreds of

This 1739 drawing by Bishop Roberts depicts the busy Charleston waterfront.

miles away from the nearest populated city, Charleston was the only English walled city in North America, rivaling the French walled city in Quebec and Spain's St. Augustine in Florida. More importantly to the pirates, Charleston boasted a large, deep-water harbor that was filled with merchant vessels that carried goods in and out of the city.

Two shipping channels linked the harbor with the open ocean. The smaller channel hugged Sullivan's Island, and the larger, main channel ran just off the beach of Morris Island. The *Revenge* sat off the bar between the two channels and waited. They did not have to wait long. A brigantine from Boston was spotted by the pirates, and the Jolly Roger was run up the mast. The brigantine's captain, Thomas Porter, was in no position to resist the pirates and quickly surrendered. The pirates were disappointed to find no valuable cargo onboard, but they did detain the vessel so her crew could not alert the citizens of Charleston. Their disappointment was short-lived as a sloop was seen arriving from the south. The sloop's captain, Joseph Palmer, also had no interest in trying to fight off or evade the pirates and promptly surrendered. The sloop was with filled valuable sugar, rum and slaves. Unfortunately for the crew of the captured sloop, they were also from Barbados, and Captain Palmer and Stede recognized each other. This sloop would be meeting the same fate as the *Turbet*, but not before sailing north with the *Revenge* and the brigantine to the Cape Fear River in North Carolina. The pirates would be using their two newly captured prizes to careen the hull of the *Revenge*.

In warm tropical and semitropical waters, barnacle, worms and other aquatic parasites attach themselves to the hulls of wooden vessels and bore tiny holes. This was not only a threat to the integrity of a wooden vessel's hull but it also reduced vessel speed. The *Revenge* slipped into the shallows of the Cape Fear River and ran onto the shore at high tide. Using the captured sloop and brigantine, the *Revenge* was hauled over first on her starboard side, exposing the hull on her port side. When the tide fell, the crew burned and scraped the barnacles off and repaired any damages. On the next tide, the *Revenge* was pulled over onto her port side, and cleaning was completed on the rest of the hull.

With the *Revenge*'s careening completed, Stede called Captain Palmer into his great cabin onboard the *Revenge*. Stede informed his hostage that he, his crew and his cargo of slaves would be transferred to Captain Porter's brigantine, and Palmer's sloop would be burned. Overcrowded and short of provisions, Porter's brigantine was released and headed south for Charleston. In an effort to delay the news of the pirates' whereabouts from reaching Charleston, much of the sails and rigging had been removed from the brigantine. A passage that should have lasted only a few days took nearly four weeks. With the crew near starvation, Captain Palmer was forced to release most of the slaves ashore into the wilds of the Carolinas before finally reaching Charleston on September 22. Captain Palmer and Captain Porter went directly to the home of South Carolina governor Robert Johnson and related the story of their capture off of Charleston nearly a month before by Stede Bonnet. Governor Johnson had only acquired his position in April of the same year. His father, Nathaniel Johnson, had served as governor from 1702 to 1709. Governor Johnson listened to Palmer's and Porter's tale and added the pirate threat of Stede Bonnet to the long list of troubles that he had inherited in Charleston that included disease, Indian wars and social unrest. Governor Johnson could not have imagined during that interview with Palmer and Porter the impact that the unlikely pirate from Barbados would have on Charleston in the future.

Now heading south towards the Straits of Florida, Stede was facing big troubles of his own. The snide and mutinous comments that had previously only been whispered by the crew behind his back were now lodged directly and openly at Stede. The crew expressed their contempt and questioned his experience and ability to hold the position of captain. Though the *Revenge* had met with success, the crew felt that it had been in spite of, and not because of, Stede's leadership. The dissenters complained that their captain had been "obliged to yield to many things that were imposed on him, during their undertaking, for want of a competent knowledge in maritime affairs." The position of captain on a pirate ship was generally voted upon by the crew, and his authority was only absolute in time of battle. The captain could be deposed at any time through a unanimous crew vote. But the unprecedented nature of the arrangement onboard the *Revenge* of the salaried crew and Stede's sole ownership of their ship blurred the line between pirate and employee. Stede responded to the crew's dissatisfaction by dispensing punishments. The slightest infractions and insubordinations now met with lashings in front of the assembled crew. But management through fear and intimidation was even less effective, and morale onboard the *Revenge* sank even lower just as the pirates were about to face their greatest challenge.

The *Revenge* passed near the Spanish wrecks and braced against the current of the Florida Straits. Stede prowled the quarterdeck, leering at his malcontented crew. Fearful of leaving the deck lest the crew descend into mutiny, he had not slept much the last few days. He was tired, and his mind was not clear. Certain that action and the capture of a prize would relieve the tension and renew the crew's trust in him, Stede was anxious to sight another vessel. When the call of "Sail to starboard!" came from the bowsprit, he did not hesitate to give the command to make all sail and close on the ship. A closer approach showed that she flew the flag of Spain. Spirits rose on the *Revenge* as the guns were run out and the Jolly Roger hoisted to the top of the mast. Stede hoped that the sight of his black flag and guns would once again prove intimidating enough for his prey to surrender. But his hopes were dashed when the Spanish vessel also ran out her guns. This was no merchant vessel but a Spanish man of war, probably sent to patrol the nearby Spanish wrecks and run off any English marauders that were diving for gold and silver. When the helmsman began to turn the wheel hard to port and steer away from the Spanish vessel, Stede stopped him and gave the order to attack. On the deck of the *Revenge*, the crew exchanged sharp looks of disbelief and fear. It seemed that everyone onboard except Stede knew that to engage a Spanish man of war was a foolish and possibly suicidal mission. Shouts of protest were curtly overruled by Stede. The pirates came alongside and as Stede was about to give the order to fire, the Spanish cannons erupted with their first broadside into the *Revenge*. The impact rocked every timber of the *Revenge*. Enveloped in smoke and splinters of wood, Stede fell to the deck. Numb and deafened by the roar of the cannons, he rolled on his side and looked out across the deck at a macabre scene. The dead and dying still at their gun stations twitched and slumped over cannons and rigging. Limbless torsos and bodies pierced by splinters of wood littered the deck. Those who had survived the broadside fired at the Spanish, but the enemy vessel had turned onto the stern of the *Revenge*. A wooden ship was most vulnerable when fired upon longitudinally,

The iconic Howard Pyle engraving *Walking the Plank*. Although popular in books and movies, there are few records of any pirates forcing their captives to walk the plank.

as gunpowder was stored in a compartment in the belly of the vessel. A well-placed shot from stern to bow could easily strike and ignite the gunpowder, destroying a vessel. Still lying on the deck, Stede saw the flash of the Spanish guns as they fired again, and he heard the crash of glass as his aft cabin windows shattered. The deck under him seemed to swell as the hot shot passed between him and the keel. The *Revenge*'s gunpowder magazine did not ignite, but the shot screamed below deck, tearing through bodies and bulkheads. Blood streamed into his eyes, and he felt the sliver of wood that was lodged in his head. Stede rubbed his head, looked at the dark, red blood covering his hand and collapsed unconscious.

When he awoke, Stede was in his shattered cabin, lying in his bed. All was quiet. Shards of glass, splinters of wood and shreds of his precious books covered the floor. Blood-caked bandages covered his head, and he felt the taut, newly sewn stitches in his scalp. Stede wondered how the *Revenge* had escaped and how long he had been unconscious. He tried to sit up but did not have the strength. A voice came from the door of his cabin, and although he could not see the face from his prone position, the message was clear and concise: half of the crew was either dead or wounded, and the *Revenge* was making for the refuge of Nassau.

# 3

# Blackbeard

Gazing at the Nassau waterfront from the deck of the *Revenge*, Stede had to wonder if his piratical career was finished. Any remaining faith and respect that the crew had in their captain was lost after their disastrous engagement with the Spanish vessel. Most of the crew had deserted the ship to the taverns and brothels of Nassau. The story of the wealthy gentleman who decided to play pirate was already a joke being toasted by pirates all over the island. The *Revenge* was terribly damaged—sails were tattered, rigging destroyed and timbers and spars splintered.

His drunken crew ashore had already begun signing articles with other pirate captains. Leaving behind their salaried life onboard the *Revenge*, Stede's crew now followed the traditional pirate code and signed articles. These articles defined the percentage of plunder each man received when taking a prize. The articles also outlined rules to be abided by onboard and punishment for infractions. An early insurance policy that covered pirates in case of injury was also created. The most detailed set of pirate articles that have survived are from the *Royal Fortune* in 1721, of which Bartholomew Roberts was captain. Roberts was a bit of a dandy and a teetotaler, so the rules onboard his vessel were probably a little more stringent than those of his peers, but the tenets of articles onboard other pirate vessels were similar:

> *I. Every man has a Vote in Affairs of Monument, has equal Title to the fresh Provisions, or strong Liquors, at any Time seized, & use them at pleasure, unless a Scarcity make it necessary, for the good of all, to Vote a Retrenchment.*

*II. Every man to be called fairly in turn, by List, on Board of Prizes, because they there on these Occasions allow'd a Shift of Cloaths: But if they defrauded the Company to the Value of a Dollar, in Plate, Jewels, or Money, MAROONING was their punishment.*

*III. No Person to game at Cards or Dice for Money.*

*IV. The Lights & Candles to be put out at eight o'Clock at Night. If any of the Crew, after that Hour, still remained inclined for Drinking, they were to do it on the open Deck.*

*V. To Keep their Piece, Pistols, & Cutlash clean, & fit for Service.*

*VI. No Boy or Woman to be allow'd amongst them. If any Man were found seducing any of the latter Sex, and carried her to Sea, disguised, he was to suffer Death.*

*VII. To Desert the Ship, or their Quarters in Battle, was punished with Death, or Marooning.*

*VIII. No striking one another on Board, but every Man's Quarrels to be ended on shore, at Sword & Pistol Thus: The Quarter-Master of the Ship, when the Parties will not come to any Reconciliation, accompanies them on Shore with what Assistance he thinks proper, & turns the Disputants Back to Back, at so many Paces, Distance. At the Word of Command, they turn and fire immediately, (or else the Piece is knocked out of their Hands). If both miss, they come to their Cutlasses, and then he is declared Victor who draws first Blood.*

*IX. No Man to talk of breaking up their Way of Living, till each has shared one thousand pounds sterling. If in order to this, any Man shall lose a Limb, or become a Cripple in their Service, he has to have eight hundred Dollars, out of publick Stock, and for lesser Hurts, proportionably.*

*X. The Captain and Quarter-Master to receive two Share of a Prize; the Master, Boatswain, & gunner, one Share and a half and other Officers, one and a Quarter.*

*XI. The Musicians to have Rest on the Sabbath Day, but the other six Days and Nights, none without special Favour.*

Overwhelmed with depression, Stede, bandaged and still in his dressing gown, sulked in his cabin. A knock came from his door. Stede, turning away from the book in his hand, saw a huge figure in the doorway. Standing over six feet tall, the figure strode into the cabin, greeted Stede and courteously addressed him as "Captain Bonnet." His piercing eyes were the only visible part of his face, which was covered by a thick, bushy beard. Strands of his beard were braided and the ends tied with ribbons. His beard was "black, which he suffered to grow of an extravagant length; as to the breadth it came up to his eyes." Silken bandoliers that suspended two pistols each were draped over his broad shoulders.

No introduction was necessary for Stede. He recognized the man from descriptions in newspaper reports of piracy that he had read while still in Barbados. This was Edward Thatch—better known as Blackbeard. Stede was star-struck.

Blackbeard had entered the piracy trade in the traditional way. Formerly a privateer, Blackbeard transitioned into piracy at the end of Queen Anne's War. As a privateer, he had sailed out of Jamaica, but as Captain Johnson describes in *A General History of Pirates*, while a privateer, "though he had often distinguished himself for uncommon boldness and personal courage, he was never raised to any command." Edward Thatch would not flourish and show his potential until he turned pirate.

Blackbeard learned quickly that bravery and skill with a cutlass and pistol were not the only tools required to be a successful pirate. He was an early student of psychological warfare. His hulking body and thick beard were already menacing enough, but at time of battle, Blackbeard would enhance his frightening image by tucking fuses made of hemp cord under the brim of his hat. Dipped in a solution of saltpeter and lime water, these fuses would burn very slowly when lit, curling thick wisp of smoke around his face, creating a demon-like visage. Stories circulated of the "devil incarnate," both true and exaggerated, and Blackbeard was happy to cultivate his fearsome reputation. Captain Johnson tells this story:

> *For being one day at sea, and little flushed with drink, "Come," says he, "let us make a hell of our own, and try how long we can bear it." Accordingly he, with two or three others, went down into the hold, and closing up the hatches, filled several pots full of brimstone and other combustible matter, and set it on fire, and so continued until they were almost suffocated, when some of the men cried out for air. At length, he opened the hatches, not a little pleased that he had held out the longest.*

Blackbeard served his pirate apprenticeship under one of the eldest and most respected pirates of Nassau, Benjamin Hornigold. Refusing to accept that Queen Anne's War had come to an end, Hornigold pursued his own personal war against the French and Spanish through piracy. By 1715, Hornigold was making sorties in the waters around the Bahamas and Cuba onboard his large sloop, narcissistically named *Benjamin*. In the spring of

The infamous Blackbeard. Note the slow-burning fuses protruding from under his hat that gave Blackbeard a frightening, devil-like appearance.

1716, the *Benjamin* captured the French merchant vessel *Marianne* and seized more than twelve thousand pounds sterling. Further successes followed, and Hornigold soon joined forces with the infamous Black Sam Bellamy, who was given command of the *Marianne*. Blackbeard and Bellamy would become very close friends, and Bellamy would serve as Blackbeard's mentor. In short order, Hornigold and Bellamy added the pirate La Bouche and his ship to their armada. Presenting an unequaled pirate force, they began hunting for prizes around Cuba. It must have made for an interesting dynamic between Hornigold and La Bouche, as Hornigold would not attack English vessels, restricting his prizes to only those of England's traditional enemies—France and Spain. La Bouche was, of course, French. Whatever their differences, the pirate consortium was hugely successful, and under their leadership, Blackbeard honed his pirate skills.

Blackbeard was devastated when, in spring 1717, he learned that Bellamy had drowned in a storm off of Cape Cod. Bellamy had sailed north without Hornigold and Blackbeard to show off his newly captured flag ship *Whydah* to his sweetheart Mary Hallett. The catastrophic storm killed all but nine of his crew. The survivors managed to crawl ashore, where they were quickly arrested and imprisoned in Boston. When word of the survivors being hanged reached Blackbeard, he was infuriated

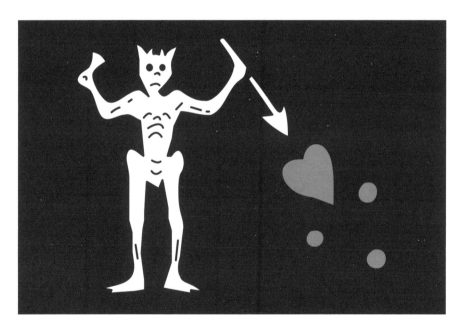

Blackbeard's flag.

and swore that he would destroy any ship that he encountered from New England. By this time, Hornigold had given Blackbeard command of his own sloop of six guns. A report received by South Carolina governor Robert Daniell (Robert Johnson's predecessor) in March 1717 regarding pirate vessel activity in Nassau stated, "Five pirates made ye harbour of Providence their place of rendezvous vizt. Hornigold, a sloop with ten guns and about eighty men; Jennings, a sloop with ten guns and one hundred men; Burgiss, a sloop with eight guns and about eighty men; White, in a small vessel with thirty men and small arms; Thatch, a sloop with six guns and about seventy men."

Shortly before Stede's ignominious arrival in Nassau, Hornigold had decided to retire from the piracy business. His insistence on not attacking English vessels did not sit well with his crew, and a vote had removed him from his position as commodore of the pirate armada. Content to rest of his laurels and spend his amassed fortune, Hornigold returned with Blackbeard to the sanctuary of Nassau. When the *Revenge* limped into the Nassau harbor, Hornigold agreed that Stede's sloop would make the perfect flagship for his apprentice. Interviews with the *Revenge*'s crew in Nassau's taverns proved the precarious state that Stede now found himself in. Blackbeard formulated a plan to take advantage of the gentleman pirate's misfortunes.

There are no records of the conversation between Blackbeard and Stede that day onboard the *Revenge*. Stede, already in a fragile state, was certainly intimidated and fearful of his guest. But Blackbeard put Stede at ease and listened sympathetically to the Barbadian planter's story. The fearsome pirate showed compassion on this occasion, and the pair brokered an unlikely bargain. Blackbeard would provide new crewmembers for the *Revenge*. He would send over his carpenters to repair the damaged sloop and his surgeon to tend to the wounded. Blackbeard would hand over command of his own sloop to his lieutenant, Richards, and Blackbeard would assume command of the *Revenge*, but only until Stede recovered from his appreciable wounds. Stede could still occupy the great stern cabin of the captain.

Stede couldn't help but feel excitement at the change in his luck. Just that morning, he was sure that his pirate career was over, and now he would be sailing with a pirate legend whose exploits and adventures he had read about and been inspired by just a few months prior while still in Barbados.

Historians have often pondered why Blackbeard was congenial in his dealings with Stede. Blackbeard certainly could have forcefully taken the *Revenge* and evicted her impotent owner, but he chose a conciliatory path.

Why? In his groundbreaking book *The Last Days of Black Beard the Pirate*, author Kevin Duffus relates that through his research, he has found that Blackbeard and Stede may have known each other prior to their meeting onboard the *Revenge*. Duffus dismisses the traditional viewpoint that Blackbeard was from Bristol, England. His research gives evidence that Blackbeard was actually Edward Beard, son of Captain James Beard of Charleston—the Beards having emigrated from Barbados to the Carolinas. While reviewing the will of Thomas Bonnet, Stede's uncle, Duffus found listed those who would benefit from Stede's uncle's estate. Among those listed was a servant named William Beard, conceivably brother of Captain James Beard and thus uncle of Blackbeard. It is possible that Blackbeard's uncle had come to Barbados as an indentured servant for Stede's uncle. Although difficult to prove, a family connection between Blackbeard and Stede does offer a reasonable explanation for the odd couple joining forces at Nassau in September 1717.

With repairs completed and two additional cannons added to the *Revenge*, the two pirate sloops weighed anchor in mid-September and headed north towards the capes of Delaware Bay. The combined vessels consisted of nearly 150 pirates. Initially, the partnership between Blackbeard and Stede seemed to be a success. Blackbeard commanded from the quarterdeck of the *Revenge* while Stede, in his dressing gown and socked feet, rested and read his precious books. Blackbeard seems to have at least feigned to involve Stede in the decision-making and management of the *Revenge*, but in regards to the sloop's captaincy, Blackbeard diplomatically advised Stede that "as he had not been used to the fatigues and care of such a post, it would be better for him to decline it and live easy, at his pleasure, in such a ship as his, where he should not be obliged to perform duty, but follow his own inclinations."

Sailing north, the *Revenge* captured the *Betty* off the coast of Virginia. Virginia's lieutenant governor Alexander Spotswood wrote of the pirate's attack "on or about the twenty-ninth day of September in the Year Afforsaid [1717] in an Hostile manner with Force and Arms on the high seas near Cape Charles in this Colony within the Jurisdiction of the Admiralty of this Court attack and force a Sloop Calld the Betty of Virginia...and the said Sloop did then and there Rob and plunder of Certain Pipes of Medera Wine and other Goods and Merchandise." With the crew's spirit emboldened by the pilfered wine, they continued north.

Reaching the busy capes of Delaware Bay, a three-week rampage ensued that included the capture of at least eighteen vessels. Free from the constraints of his old-fashioned mentor Benjamin Hornigold and embittered at the citizens of New England for the hanging of Bellamy's crew, Blackbeard and his crew did not discriminate as to which nation a prize belonged to, and his crew was wantonly malicious toward its captives. The *Boston News Letter* carried the story of a Captain Codd "from Liverpool and Dublin with 150 Passengers, many whereof are Servants. He was taken twelve days since off our Cape by a Pirate Sloop called *Revenge*, of twelve guns, 150 Men, Commanded by one Teach, who Formerly Sail'd Mate out of this Port." The story continues that the pirates "threw all Codd's Cargo over board, excepting some small matters they fancied." Captain Goelet's vessel from Curacao bound for Philadelphia was captured, and her cargo of cocoa thrown into the ocean. Newspaper articles also mentioned Stede's diminished role onboard his own ship. In the same article that told the story of the unfortunate Captain Codd , the *Boston News-Letter* wrote:

> On board the Pirate Sloop is Major Bennet, but has no Command, he walks about in his Morning Gown, and then to his Books, of which he has a good Library on Board, he was not well of his wounds that he received by attacking a Spanish Man of War, which kill'd and wounded thirty to forty men. After which putting into Providence, the place of Rendevouze for the Pirates, they put the afore said Capt. Teach on board for this Cruise.

"Major Bennet" was, of course, Stede Bonnet.

The *Revenge*'s rampage continued, and it captured more vessels, including prizes from St. Lucia, Antigua and New York. But as the late-October wind grew cold, Blackbeard decided to head south to warmer waters. In one of history's quirky twists of fate, the *Revenge*, sailing south, passed close to the warship HMS *Lyme* off the Virginia Capes. Less than a year later, the *Lyme*'s Captain Brand and Governor Spotswood would be outlining a plan to capture or kill Blackbeard.

The *Revenge* bypassed the Bahamas, en route to the Lesser Antilles. Stede had suitably recovered from his wounds, but his entreaties to his restoration as captain of the *Revenge* were brushed off by Blackbeard. Stede's stress was amplified as the *Revenge* steered a course uncomfortably close to Barbados. He began to sense that he had been taken advantage of by Blackbeard. He was just a means to an end and wondered if he would ever command his beloved *Revenge* again. But fate would intervene in Stede's favor.

Alexander Spotswood.

In mid-November, while the *Revenge* lay off of the island of Martinique, a sail was spotted, and Blackbeard gave the order to intercept. The vessel turned out to be the slave ship *La Concorde* from Nantes, France. Originally built as a privateer, *La Concorde* was a large vessel of two hundred tons, with sixteen mounted cannons. She carried a cargo of over four hundred slaves. *La Concorde*'s captain, Dosset, was just completing a nightmarish transatlantic journey. The crew suffered from dysentery and scurvy, and only half were even healthy enough to stand their watches. Although she outgunned the *Revenge*, *La Concorde*'s crew was in no condition to fight the pirates. She quickly struck her colors and surrendered. Dosset, the crew and their human cargo were put ashore on the remote island of Bequia. Over the next couple of weeks, Blackbeard refitted and converted *La Concorde* into his new flagship. He mounted additional cannons, bringing her total to as many as forty guns. With a nod to his privateering days and his Jacobite leanings, Blackbeard renamed her *Queen Anne's Revenge*. Stede was unceremoniously restored to captain of the *Revenge*, and the vessels set a northwest course to the waters between St. Vincent and St. Lucia.

Sailing comfortably in the wake of *Queen Anne's Revenge*, Stede's fears began to abate as the *Revenge* sailed away from Barbados. He was master of his own sloop again and partnered with the most-feared pirate in the Caribbean. The unlikely team began to prey on merchant vessel traffic around the sugar islands of the Grenadine chain of the Windward Islands. The *Great Allen* from Boston was captured in late November. Her captain, Taylor, was put in irons and whipped to try to extract information as to any hidden money onboard. The *Boston News Letter* reports that "the pirates plundered her of what they thought fit, put all their men ashore upon [St. Vincent], and then set fire to the ship." Blackbeard was still honoring his oath to destroy any New England vessels that he encountered. The *Margaret* was captured off of Anguilla, and the pirates removed her cargo of cattle

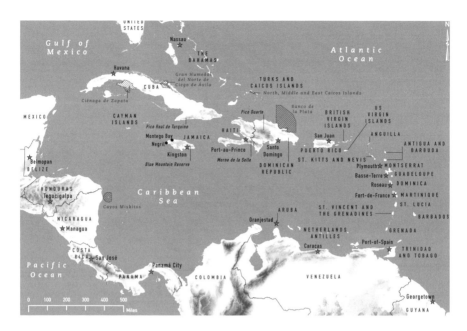

A map of the Caribbean.

and hogs before heading north to Nevis. Lying in the harbor at Nevis was the thirty-gun warship HMS *Scarborough*. The crew of the *Queen Anne's Revenge* was anxious to engage the *Scarborough* and test the power of Blackbeard's new flagship. However, Blackbeard had taken ill and overruled any plans to match broadsides with the royal warship. Stede must have breathed a sigh of relief. The *Scarborough*'s home station was Bridgetown, Barbados. Had he been captured in the proposed engagement with the *Scarborough*, Stede would certainly have been delivered back to Barbados to face trial and certain death by hanging in front of his family and neighbors.

Historical records are quiet about the pirate's activities in the winter of 1717–18. However, Colin Woodard, author of *Republic of Pirates*, discovered an issue of *Weekly Journal or British Gazetter* that reports that a pirate ship of forty guns, known to Spanish mariners as the "Great Devil," was lurking in the waters of the Campeche Bank. This "Great Devil" could have only been Blackbeard.

By late March, Blackbeard and Stede moved into the Bay of Honduras and decided to separate to cover more territory. The *Revenge* sailed south to the Bay Islands. Near Roatan Island, the twenty-six-gun, four-hundred-ton merchant ship *Protestant Caesar* from Boston was spotted. Although outgunned by the enormous vessel, Stede was anxious to prove his mettle, and as the sun set, he gave the order to attack. Those onboard who had survived the disastrous engagement with the Spanish man of war over seven months prior must have been overcome with an eerie sense of déjà vu. Remembering the lessons of that bloody day, Stede maneuvered the *Revenge* onto the vulnerable stern of the *Protestant Caesar* and fired her starboard-side cannons. The *Protestant Caesar* responded with her stern-mounted cannons. Small arms fire broke out as the two vessels edged precariously close to one another. Stede brazenly called out for the Boston merchantmen to surrender and warned that if he was fired upon again, he would give no quarter to the *Protestant Caesar*'s crew. Unimpressed, the *Protestant Caesar*'s captain, William Wyer, ordered his cannons to fire again. The two vessels engaged in a running fight, exchanging broadsides past midnight until Stede finally called off the pursuit.

The exhausted and battered crew of the *Revenge* voted to head back north and rendezvous with Blackbeard. They found the *Queen Anne's Revenge* at anchor at Turneffe. With his tail between his legs, Stede reported to Blackbeard the failed attack on the *Protestant Caesar*. A council meeting was held, and the pirates decided that the attack on the superior *Protestant Caesar* was a foolish decision on Stede's part and that he should be removed from command of the *Revenge*. Blackbeard's faithful lieutenant Richards was given command of the *Revenge*, and Stede, like a scolded schoolboy, retreated below deck of the *Queen Anne's Revenge*.

Blackbeard was not about to let a vessel from Boston get the better of him and determined to head south in pursuit of the *Protestant Caesar*. Before they sailed, the unfortunate logwood cutting vessel *Adventure* sailed into the lagoon at Turneffe to take on freshwater. The *Adventure* was quickly captured, and Blackbeard decided to add the sloop to his growing armada. The *Adventure*'s Captain David Herriot and most of his crew decided to join the *Queen Anne's Revenge*'s company rather than be left ashore at Turneffe. Blackbeard placed Israel Hands in command of the *Adventure*. Arriving off Honduras on April 8, the pirates found the *Protestant Caesar* at anchor. The spirit and boldness that Captain Wyer and his crew displayed against the twelve-gun *Revenge* was lost when confronted with the forty-gun *Queen Anne's Revenge*. Wyer and his crew quickly lowered their longboats into the water and beat a hasty retreat to the jungles ashore. Hidden in the mangroves, the *Protestant Caesar*'s crew watched as the pirates picked their vessel clean. Blackbeard sent a message to Captain Wyer stating that if he would come aboard the pirate flagship for a meeting, no harm would come to him or his crew. A terrified Wyer came aboard the *Queen Anne's Revenge* and entered the great cabin of the captain. Blackbeard explained that the good news was that the crew would remain unharmed, but the bad news was that because she was from Boston, the *Protestant Caesar* would have to be burned. Safely back on the beach, Wyer and his crew watched the pirate flotilla sail away as their ship burned to the waterline.

Blackbeard plotted a course for Nassau. A veritable prisoner onboard the *Queen Anne's Revenge*, Stede found a sympathetic friend in David Herriot, the hapless former captain of the *Adventure*. Stede explained to his new friend that he was ready to leave the pirate life. Arriving in Nassau, Stede received news that he initially hoped could be his salvation. In response to the flood of complaints and requests for protection by merchants and officials throughout the English colonies, King George I had issued a royal pardon to pirates on September 5, 1717. (See Appendix I for a copy of the King's pardon.) The proclamation offered immunity from prosecution to any pirate who surrendered himself to a government official by September 5, 1718. The rumor among the pirates was that a new governor carrying the pardon was sailing from England to Nassau, offering amnesty to those who accepted the pardon and hanging those who would not. However, Stede's hopes for escape from his piratical career were dashed when he learned that the pardon applied to only those acts of piracy committed before January 5. His botched attack on the *Protestant Caesar* had come after the grace period of the royal pardon.

In Nassau, Blackbeard supervised the refitting and resupplying of his growing armada of vessels. A small supply ship was added to the consortium as more pirates signed articles with Blackbeard. By the time the four vessels sailed two weeks later, Blackbeard commanded nearly four hundred pirates. The group prowled the waters around the familiar Spanish wrecks off Florida but found little. Most of the treasure had already been salvaged in the more than two and a half years since the hurricane had sunk the treasure fleet. A council meeting was held onboard the *Queen Anne's Revenge* to decide where next to hunt. Resigned to his life as a pirate, Stede raised his voice and recounted his success over eight months prior at the busy port of Charleston. The articulate Stede enchanted the assembled pirates with his tales of the easy pickings in the waters off the walled city. The vote was unanimous, and by late May, the *Queen Anne's Revenge*, the *Revenge*, the *Adventure* and the newly added supply ship were sitting off the bar of Charleston.

# 4

# Blockade of Charleston

Unaware of the pirate threat looming off their coast, the roughly four thousand souls inside the walls of Charleston already had a litany of issues to contend with. A hurricane in 1713 had nearly decimated the city, and nearly five years later, repairs were still ongoing. War with the surrounding Native American tribes had killed hundreds of colonists throughout South Carolina. Beginning in 1715, the Yemassee War had caused the population of Charleston to swell as refugees from the countryside abandoned their farms and sought the protection of the walled city. Food and supplies were stretched dangerously thin. Funding the war against the Native American tribes had nearly bankrupted the colony. Tragically, an unfortunate outbreak of yellow fever also swept through Charleston, killing hundreds more. Most of the citizens blamed their problems on the Lord Proprietors in England who controlled South Carolina. Like absentee, miserly landlords, the Lord Proprietors were slow or even reluctant to offer aid and protection to their fledgling colony. An appointed governor was in place in Charleston, but the position was generally ineffective as he had little authority or power and had to defer most decisions to the Lord Proprietors. A message sent from Charleston to England could take more than four months before a response was received, and unfortunately for Charleston's citizens, the answer was too often "no."

Into Charleston's governmental authority vacuum stepped Colonel William Rhett. Born in London in 1666, the ambitious and enterprising Rhett arrived in Charleston in 1694. An unrivaled civic and military

Colonel William Rhett. A remarkable civic and military leader of Charleston, Rhett led a fleet that repelled a combined French and Spanish force in 1706.

leader, he served in his lifetime as commissioner of fortifications and Indian trade, deputy surveyor of customs and Speaker of the Common House of Assembly as well as being a militia officer and skilled mariner. He also served as warden and treasurer of his beloved St. Phillip's Church. Rhett and his wife, Sarah, had become very wealthy merchants, and Rhett owned a large wharf that serviced vessels calling at Charleston. Near the foot of Rhett's wharf, close to the present-day intersection of Queen and East Bay Streets, the couple owned a townhome, but by 1707, Rhett had built a large house outside the city walls on twenty-eight acres of land that he named Rhettsbury.

William Rhett had sealed his reputation as the hero and defender of Charleston in August 1706, when a combined French and Spanish fleet arrived in Charleston harbor. The powerful force consisted of the frigate *Soleil* of twenty-two cannons, four smaller sloops and a galley. On board the ships were almost seven hundred Spanish soldiers and two hundred Indian allies. Under a flag of truce, a French officer was brought before Governor Nathaniel Johnson, where the Frenchman boldly demanded the surrender of the city. Governor Johnson flatly refused, and the officer was escorted back to the waterfront. Legend says that as the French officer was being led through the city back to his longboat, the small Charleston militia assembled along the road before the French officer. As the officer passed, the militia would scramble behind buildings and side streets to present themselves again at another location, creating the false illusions that the city was well manned and defended. Meanwhile, preparations were underway to assemble a fleet of armed merchant vessels to repel the enemy fleet. William Rhett was named vice admiral by Governor Johnson, and he assumed command of the flagship *Crown Galley*, with twelve guns. Five other vessels—the *Mermaid*, *Richard*, *William*, *Flying Horse* and *Seaflower*—joined the fleet that, in total, consisted of more than thirty guns and three hundred men. The Charleston fleet set sail into the harbor on

August 31. The sight of the armed merchant fleet (and possibly the reports of the city's defenses by the duped French officer) proved too much for the enemy, and the Franco-Spanish vessels fled the harbor without firing a shot. Rhett returned to a hero's welcome in Charleston.

However, Rhett was not without his detractors. Holding the position of deputy surveyor of customs while also being a merchant and owner of a large wharf was considered by many to be a blatant conflict of interest. Rhett had been accused of abusing his government title by offering favors to vessels that used his wharf and services. This "conflict of interest" led to open hostilities in 1716 between Rhett and then governor Robert Daniell. Daniell had commissioned a Captain Matthew Husson to hunt pirates around Florida and the Bahamas. When the prize *Betty* was brought by Husson into Charleston harbor, a dispute of jurisdiction over the prize between Rhett and Governor Daniell exploded and divided the city. Rhett believed that as deputy surveyor of customs, he should have access to the prize to ensure that the Crown received its fair

Colonel William Rhett's house at 54 Hasell Street, built circa 1712, is considered to be one of the oldest homes in Charleston. Located only a few blocks north of bustling Market Street in downtown Charleston, the house originally sat outside the city's walls on twenty-eight acres of land called Rhettsbury. *Photo by author*.

portion. Governor Daniell contested that the prize had come from his commission to Captain Husson and denied Rhett access to the vessel under threat of arrest. Rhett ignored Daniell's threats and boarded the *Betty*, loading confiscated goods into his longboat to deliver to his wharf. Enraged, Daniell called out the militia. Seeking protection, Rhett steered his longboat toward the Royal Navy warship HMS *Shoreham* anchored in the harbor. Daniell called for Rhett to return with the *Betty*'s cargo, but Rhett ignored him. Daniell ordered the militia to open fire. Rhett was struck in the chest but survived the injury. The *Betty*'s cargo was eventually returned to Daniell, but the remainder of his term as governor was uneasy in the wake of the conflict with Rhett.

The threat of the Franco-Spanish fleet of 1706 had shown Charleston's vulnerability by sea, and foremost among the citizens' requests to the Lord Proprietors had been a Royal Navy presence to defend the city against the Spanish and French, as well as pirates. As discussed in an earlier chapter, the speaker of the House of Assembly in Charleston, George Logan, formally requested in 1716 that the Royal Navy warship HMS *Shoreham* remain in Charleston to offer protection from pirates, but the request was denied. As rice became the major cash crop, Charleston had begun to flourish economically. Rice was not a popular food source in the English diet, so exported rice was sailing to foreign ports around the world. The imports that rice profits brought back into the city were being intercepted by the pirates lingering offshore. Stede was not the only pirate who had already profited from the busy trade lanes in and out of Charleston. The infamous Christopher Moody, in command of two pirate vessels, had captured several vessels off the Charleston bar shortly after Stede's departure in August 1717. More recently, the fearsome Charles Vane had preyed on vessels inbound to Charleston. The loss of goods at sea, however, was not the people's greatest fear. Their greatest fear was of a pirate invasion. As the number of pirates around Charleston mushroomed, the fear was that if several pirate crews banded together, they could sail into the harbor and sack and burn the city. In its weakened state and with no naval presence, the city was greatly dependent on its defensive walls for protection.

With the nearby threat of Spanish-held Florida, the earliest settlers of Charleston had wasted little time in building defenses. By the early eighteenth century, Charleston was comprised of a walled fortress approximately one mile wide by a half mile deep. The walls ran roughly north to south from present-day Cumberland Street to Water Street and east to west from East Bay Street to Meeting Street. The popular Market Street of today was a

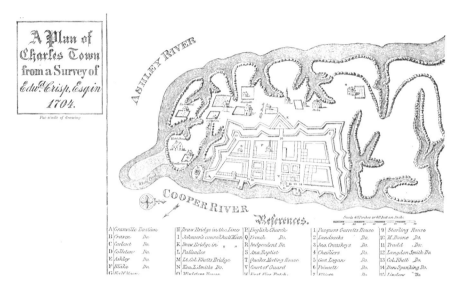

Edward Crisp's 1704 map of the walled city of Charleston.

creek that provided a natural moat for the northern wall, and Water Street, until the early nineteenth century, was the location of Vanderhorst Creek. Six diamond-shaped bastions dotted the works with smaller triangle-shaped redoubts positioned between them. All were armed with cannons of various sizes and calibers. At the foot of Broad Street, facing the Cooper River and the expanse of the harbor, was the Half Moon Battery, which contained the Court of Guard building. The Half Moon Battery was the center of defense for Charleston and although heavily armed, its guns did not have the range to reach an enemy five miles away at the Charleston bar.

Blackbeard and his four vessels lingering at the Charleston bar had wasted no time. The Charleston pilot boat, which guided vessels over the treacherous Charleston bar, was quickly captured. Over a five-day period, eight other vessels were captured. News quickly reached a panicked Charleston, and no vessel dared sail out of the harbor. One of the vessels captured was the *Crowley*, commanded by Captain Robert Clark. The *Crowley* was full of passengers bound for London who were quickly taken onboard the *Queen Anne's Revenge* and interrogated. Among the *Crowley's* passengers was Samuel Wragg, a wealthy Charleston merchant and member of the Carolina Provincial Council. He was traveling to London, accompanied by his four-year-old-son, William, to meet with the Lord Proprietors to request financial aid for the struggling city. Blackbeard was delighted to have such a valuable hostage. With the questioning complete, Wragg and the rest of the hostages were returned to the *Crowley* and abruptly thrown into the dark hold of the ship. Blackbeard called a council meeting of the pirates onboard the *Queen Anne's Revenge*, while the passengers huddled in the dark and feared the worst. An hour later, the hatch cover was removed, and the hostages were again shuttled back to the *Queen Anne's Revenge* to be addressed by Blackbeard.

Blackbeard informed the frightened hostages that the council had unanimously voted to send two pirates into Charleston to deliver a list of demands to Governor Johnson. To assure delivery of the ransom and the safe return of the messengers, all of the hostages would be kept prisoners onboard the *Queen Anne's Revenge*. Should any harm come to his pirates while ashore, all of the hostages would be put to death and their heads sent to the governor.

Assuming the role of spokesperson for the hostages, Samuel Wragg addressed Blackbeard.

The Old Exchange and Provost Dungeon in Charleston stands at the location of the Half Moon Battery of the original walled city. *Photo courtesy of the Old Exchange and Provost Dungeon, 122 East Bay Street, Charleston.*

*He proposed that one of them might go with the two gentlemen that were to be sent on the embassy, who might truly represent the danger they were in, and induce them more readily to submit, in order to save the lives of so many of the King's subjects, and further, to prevent any insult from the common people (for whose conduct on such an occasion, they could not answer) on the person of his envoys.*

Wragg offered to accompany the two messengers, leaving his son behind as proof of his commitment to the successful completion of the pirates' mission. But the savvy Blackbeard was not going to release his most valuable hostage. A passenger from the *Crowley* named Mr. Marks was chosen instead. Marks and his two pirate companions were given exactly two days to return with the requested ransom. Blackbeard threatened that if there were any treachery by the citizens of Charleston that he would "come over the barr for to burn the ships that lay before the Towne, and to beat it about [its] ears." Watching from the deck of the *Queen Anne's Revenge*, the hostages anxiously watched the trio row the longboat towards Charleston.

Two days passed without any news from the delegation that had been sent ashore. Enraged, Blackbeard paced the deck and stared toward the city. The *Crowley's* hostages were called on deck, where Blackbeard informed the terrified prisoners that, clearly, the governor in Charleston placed little value on the lives of its citizens and would not be delivering the ransom. He was certain that the two pirates had been arrested. Blackbeard instructed the hostages to prepare themselves for immediate death. Maintaining the cool head of a politician, Samuel Wragg spoke up and offered that there must be some unforeseen factors that had caused delay. Wragg proposed that perhaps something had happened to the delegation's boat while rowing into Charleston or maybe the governor was having difficulty locating all the items listed in the ransom. Blackbeard reluctantly agreed to wait for one more day. As the sun began to set the following day, the hostages saw a small boat coming out of the harbor towards the *Queen Anne's Revenge*. Hopes for salvation quickly dissolved when the boat contained neither the ransom nor the two pirates and their hostage. The stranger from the small boat climbed onto the *Queen Anne's Revenge* and reported to Blackbeard that he had been paid by Mr. Marks to sail out and explain the trio's delay in returning.

During their trip into Charleston, Mr. Marks and the two pirates had been caught in bad weather, and their boat had capsized. The three men swam to an uninhabited island several miles from the city (probably present-

William Wragg's monument at Westminster Abbey, London. William Wragg was only four years old when he and his father, Samuel Wragg, were taken prisoner by Blackbeard during the blockade of Charleston in 1718. William Wragg would grow up to become a well-respected public servant in Charleston. In 1771, he was offered the position of chief justice, but he declined. A devoted Loyalist, William sailed for England after South Carolina declared independence at the outset of the American Revolution. He drowned when his ship sank off the coast of Holland on September 3, 1777. *Copyright: Dean and Chapter of Westminster.*

day Morris Island). Fully aware that the lives of the *Crowley*'s hostages were dependent on his success, Mr. Marks convinced the two pirates to float a wooden hatch cover found on the island and propel the group towards Charleston by kicking through the open water of the harbor. Caught by tide and current, the exhausted group was near certain death when they were rescued by passing fishermen.

Blackbeard accepted the explanation and sent the small boat back to Charleston to inform the governor that he had two more days to supply the ransom. The hostages, by now numb with fear, returned below deck and waited and prayed.

When the two additional days had passed with no word from Charleston, Blackbeard was furious. Some of the desperate passengers offered to pilot the *Queen Anne's Revenge* into the harbor, and if an envoy with the ransom was not seen, they would stand by the pirates and help destroy the city that had betrayed them. The pirate fleet weighed anchor and sailed into the harbor within full view of the Charleston citizenry. Panic and fear spread throughout the city as annihilation seemed inevitable. But just as Blackbeard was preparing his gunners to fire the *Queen Anne's Revenge*'s forty guns into Charleston, a boat, with Mr. Marks waving frantically from the bow, was seen through Blackbeard's spyglass. Blackbeard's missing two pirates lethargically rowed the boat alongside and heaved a chest onto the deck of the *Queen Anne's Revenge*. Anxious to see what valuables had nearly cost them their lives, the hostages crowded around the ransom chest as it was opened. Wragg and his fellow hostages were shocked to see that the chest did not contain gold, silver or jewels, but instead was full of medicines, particularly mercury. It seems that Blackbeard and his pirates had been suffering from venereal diseases that were most likely picked up in the brothels of Nassau. Early eighteenth-century doctors treated venereal diseases, such as syphilis, with mercury. The effects of a venereal disease would most likely explain Blackbeard's reported illness and reluctance to attack the HMS *Scarborough* at Nevis the previous autumn.

Satisfied with the contents of the chest, Blackbeard demanded that Mr. Marks explain the delay. He related that having reached Charleston after their rescue by fishermen, arrangements for the medicines were immediately made by the governor and his council. However, Marks's two pirate companions decided to make the most of their shore leave and strutted the streets of Charleston within "the sight of all the people, who were fired with utmost indignation, looking upon them as robbers and murderers and particularly the authors of their wrongs and oppression; but durst not so much as think of executing their revenge, for fear of bringing more calamities upon themselves, and so they were forced to let the villains pass with impunity." Finding old drinking friends within the city, the two pirates went on a two-day drunken bender. When the required medicines had been assembled and Marks was prepared to return to the *Queen Anne's Revenge*, the two pirates could not be found. The entire city went on alert and began searching for the pair. Nearly two days later, the two were found in one of Charleston's taverns, fantastically drunk and only semiconscious.

*This Lean, Straight Rover Looked the Part of a Competent Soldier*, by Frank Schoonover, offers an exaggerated depiction of Blackbeard's pirates marching through the streets of Charleston during the blockade of 1718.

Wragg and the rest of the hostages were relieved of their valuables and most of their clothing and were returned half naked to the *Crowley*. The four pirate vessels sailed out of Charleston harbor and set a course for North Carolina. Staring back at the walled city from the rail of the *Queen Anne's Revenge*, Stede knew that he had been part of a monumental event. Many historians consider the blockade of Charleston to be the high tide of the Golden Age of Piracy. But like those unfortunate souls from the *Crowley*, Stede felt like Blackbeard's prisoner. Stede could not have imagined, as he watched Charleston fade into the wake of the *Queen Anne's Revenge*, the impact his role in the blockade would have on his future. Lost in thought, he was alarmed when he heard Blackbeard calling to him from the great cabin. Nervously entering Blackbeard's salon, Stede found Blackbeard to be cordial and noticed he now referred to Stede as "Captain Bonnet," just as he had at their first meeting in Nassau. Blackbeard coolly informed Stede that he would be given back command of the *Revenge*. Whether because of his health or hopes for a peaceful life, Blackbeard had decided to retire from piracy and accept the King's pardon. He encouraged Stede to do the same. Stede reminded Blackbeard that the terms of the pardon only applied to those piracies committed before January 5, and their capture of the *Protestant Caesar* and the *Adventure*, as well as their recent activities at Charleston, had occurred well outside of the pardon's statutes. Blackbeard explained that with a tribute of some barrels of sugar or molasses, Governor Charles Eden of North Carolina could be convinced to overlook the timing of their indiscretions and sign the royal pardon for both of them. In a few days, the pirate fleet would put in at Topsail Inlet (present-day Beaufort Inlet) and carcen the *Queen Anne's Revenge*'s hull, and then Blackbeard and Stede could make their way inland to North Carolina's capital at Bath to meet the governor. Blackbeard even had plans for the pair's future. The King of Denmark had renewed hostilities with Spain, so upon receiving their pardons, Blackbeard and Stede could sail to the island of St. Thomas, Denmark's foremost colony in the Caribbean, and apply for a privateer commission against Spain.

Stede's spirits were high as the *Queen Anne's Revenge* approached Topsail Inlet. Stede felt that he had been wrong about Blackbeard's past intentions and scoffed at his previous feelings that Blackbeard had seemingly taking advantage of him and his *Revenge*. In just a few days, Stede would start life with a clean slate and would again be in command of the *Revenge*.

Suddenly, Stede felt the *Queen Anne's Revenge* jolt violently. The timbers under his feet moaned and vibrated. The wind fell out of the sails, and the

Members of the North Carolina Department of Archaeology–Underwater Branch lift a cannon from the wreck of the *Queen Anne's Revenge* off of Beaufort, North Carolina. First discovered in 1996, excavation operations on the wreck are still ongoing. *Photo courtesy of the North Carolina Office of State Archaeology–Underwater Branch.*

wheel spun free in Blackbeard's hand on the quarterdeck. The ship listed hard to the starboard side, and the hysterical crew clamored up the deck to brace themselves against the railing. The great pirate flagship had run aground. Blackbeard, the normally consummate navigator, had steered the *Queen Anne's Revenge* onto a sandbar. Blackbeard called to the nearby *Adventure* to throw lines over to the stricken vessel and attempt to pull her free, but it was too late. In her death throes, Stede could hear the keel of the mighty ship crack.

The crew of the *Queen Anne's Revenge* was safely removed, and the process of moving the wrecked ship's cargo and provisions to the *Revenge* and *Adventure* began. Blackbeard told Stede to start the journey to Bath without him and apply for his pardon. Blackbeard would follow him in a few days, when the transfer of goods from the *Queen Anne's Revenge* was completed. Several barrels of sugar and molasses were loaded into a longboat to offer as a bribe to the governor. Stede and five other pirates set sail into the calm waters toward Core Sound. Stede waved back at Blackbeard standing on the shore. The two would never meet again.

# 5

# Treachery

Crossing the Core and Pamlico Sounds, Stede and his band swung west into the Pamlico River, reaching Bath a few days after departing from Topsail Inlet. South Carolina's capital in Charleston was a thriving metropolis compared to North Carolina's tiny waterfront village in Bath. Situated on Bath Creek, a tributary of the Pamlico River, the capital at the time of Stede's arrival boasted only a couple dozen homes. Governor Charles Eden presided over a colony on the brink of ruin. With a small, poor population and its own problem with aggressive Native Americans, North Carolina was nearly bankrupt. Governor Eden was more than happy to accept his visitors' gifts in exchange for his endorsements of their royal pardons. Eden also issued Stede a commission to sail with the *Revenge* to St. Thomas to seek his Letter of Marque from the island's governor.

Returning to Topsail Inlet, Stede could see the mast of the *Revenge* across the dunes. The *Queen Anne's Revenge* still lay battered and broken in the surf, but the *Adventure* was gone. Climbing onboard the *Revenge*, Stede found his ship to be eerily quiet. Walking below deck into the cargo hold, Stede's face grew pale, and his heart sank. Blackbeard had double-crossed him. All of the *Revenge*'s cargo and provisions had been removed to the *Adventure*, and Blackbeard had long sailed away. Stede's pulse raced as he was gripped with the realization that the grounding of the *Queen Anne's Revenge* had been a ruse. It was all part of an elaborate plan by Blackbeard to break up his huge company of pirates and keep all of the hard-earned plunder to himself.

Blackbeard had sprung his plan into action as soon as Stede had left for Bath to obtain his pardon. Blackbeard and approximately one hundred conspirators drew their weapons and turned on the rest of the bewildered pirate gang. Most of the betrayed pirates were left in Beaufort, but twenty-five men, comprised mostly of the crew of the captured *Adventure*, including David Herriot, were marooned on a small, uninhabited spit of sand, today called Bogues Bank, about a mile off of Beaufort, "no doubt with a design they should perish, there being no inhabitant, or provisions to subsist withal, nor any boat or materials to build or make any kind of launch or vessel, to escape from that desolate place. They remained there two nights and one day, without subsistance, or the least prospect of any, expecting nothing else but a lingering death." Tipped off by some of the pirates left in Beaufort, Stede rescued the marooned pirates.

Stede had just finished detailing his plan to sail to St. Thomas to obtain a privateering commission to his newly rescued crew of roughly thirty men when a small boat selling apples and cider approached the *Revenge*. The captain of the small boat told Stede that he had seen the *Adventure* just two days prior at anchor in Ocracoke Inlet, only a day's sail north. Stede knew there were hardly enough provisions onboard the *Revenge* to make the two-week passage to St. Thomas. A diversion north to hunt for Blackbeard would force the crew to barter or steal provisions to survive. He knew the prudent course of action was to sail south to his new life as a privateer, but the sting of Blackbeard's betrayal was overwhelming. Stroking the pocket of

*Marooned*, by Howard Pyle. Few punishments were more feared by pirates than the practice of marooning. Unless rescued, a marooned pirate could face a slow death by dehydration, starvation or exposure.

his waistcoat, he felt the folded parchment that was his royal pardon. Staring north, the passion for vengeance swept over Stede like a fever. He gave the fateful order to sail north to Ocracoke.

Stede calculated that, with the *Revenge*'s twelve guns compared to the *Adventure*'s eight guns, the odds were in his favor. Besides, the element of surprise would be on his side as his former master would never suspect that Stede would find the *Adventure*, much less engage her in battle. But sailing into the secluded Ocracoke Inlet, the crew of the *Revenge* found itself alone. Unknown to Stede, Blackbeard had passed through Ocracoke Inlet, entered the Pamlico Sound and headed to Bath to received the royal pardon. Had Stede peered over the dunes toward the ocean on his return trip from Bath to Topsail as he crossed the Pamilico and Core Sounds, he would have seen the double-crossing Blackbeard and the *Adventure* sailing north on the outer passage around the barrier islands.

Lying at anchor in Ocracoke Inlet, a council meeting was held onboard the *Revenge*. The first order of business was the unanimous vote for Robert Tucker as quartermaster. Tucker had served on a merchant vessel from Bermuda that had been captured a few months earlier by the *Queen Anne's Revenge*. Much like David Herriot and the crew of the *Adventure*, Tucker had chosen to join the ranks of his pirate captors. Tucker explained that the solution to the shortage of provisions was simple—head north to the busy trade lanes off Virginia and return to piracy. Stede vehemently protested, but the crew stood firmly with Tucker. Stede was still determined not to invalidate his pardon. He unwillingly agreed to the crew's plan but only under the terms that any vessels seized would be given compensation for any goods taken. To further distance himself from any future indiscretions, he also now insisted on being called "Captain Thomas" and renamed the *Revenge* the *Royal James*, in homage to his Jacobite sentiments.

The newly christened *Royal James* had hardly tacked out of Ocracoke Inlet when a sail was seen on the horizon, and a chase began. The pirates boarded the prize and took out some provisions, including pork and bread. Stede's mandate was honored, and the stunned crew of the captured sloop was given some molasses and rice in exchange for the provisions. Another prize bound to Glasgow was taken and some tobacco removed in exchange for more molasses and rice. However, by the time the *Royal James* arrived off the Virginia capes, the crew had abandoned Stede's practice of forced bartering with captured prizes, and an outright piratical frenzy began that included the capture of no less than thirteen merchant vessels between Virginia and New Jersey. Stede had once again lost his grip over another crew. The impetuous and brutal Robert Tucker had become captain in everything but name, and the rest of the crew now referred to him as "Father." On July 29, the fifty-ton sloop *Fortune*, bound from Philadelphia to Barbados, was captured off Cape Henlopen. Storming onboard the *Fortune* with several other pirates, Tucker "fell to beating and cutting the people with his cutlass, and cut one man's arm." Captain Thomas Read of the *Fortune* was held prisoner on the *Royal James* while his sloop was picked clean of its cargo of provisions.

Two days later, a sixty-ton sloop named the *Francis* from Antigua was seen anchored nearby. Tucker and a small band of pirates approached the *Francis* in a canoe. When the crew of the *Francis* hailed the approaching canoe and asked from where they had come, Tucker yelled back that he was Captain Thomas Read from Philadelphia and asked permission to come aboard. A rope ladder was lowered, and Tucker and his fellow pirates climbed onboard. As James Killing, first mate of the *Francis*, would later testify, "So soon as they came on board, they clapped their hands to their cutlasses, and I said we are taken." The captain of the *Francis*, Peter Manwareing, was taken by a couple of the pirates onboard the *Royal James* to present his papers and cargo manifest. The pirates that remained onboard the *Francis* held an impromptu party. Killing described the scene:

> So when they came into the cabin, the first thing they began with was the pineapples, which they cut down with their cutlasses. They asked me if I would not come and eat along with them. I told them I had but little stomach to eat. They asked me why I looked so melancholy. I told them I looked as well as I could. They asked me what liquor I had on board. I told them some rum and sugar. So they made bowls of punch and went to drinking of the Pretender's health and hoped to see him King of the English nation. Then sang a song or two.

The following morning, the *Francis* was relieved of its cargo.

By the time of the capture of the *Francis* and *Fortune*, Stede seems to have embraced the role of an outright pirate again. As he had done when he lost control of his first crew in August 1717, Stede turned to utilizing fear and intimidation to maintain his authority. Two men were ordered to be whipped before the mast for minor infractions during the capture of the *Francis* and *Fortune*. Captain Read and Captain Manwareing were called into Stede's great cabin and informed that the pair would remain prisoners and both their ships would sail in consort with the *Royal James* to the Cape Fear River in North Carolina. The *Royal James*'s hull needed to be careened again. Before sailing,

*Charleston City Paper* 2009–2010 Best Actor, Rodney Lee Rogers, performs his one-man show *The Gentleman Pirate* at the Powder Magazine (79 Cumberland Street, Charleston). *Photo by Don Lewis.*

Stede decided to dispose of some of the growing number of prisoners onboard the *Royal James*. Loading a longboat with prisoners under the guard of several pirates, Stede wrote a letter to the coastal inhabitants threatening "that if any of the inhabitants offered to hurt the hair of the head of any person belonging to his crew, he the said Bonnet would put to death and destroy all the prisoners he had on board, and would also go ashore and burn the whole town." The pirates returned unmolested.

The *Royal James* and her two prizes departed Cape Henlopen on the night of August 1. The following morning, Stede noticed that the *Francis* was slipping away from the *Royal James*'s starboard quarter. He barked through the speaking trumpet that if the crew of the *Francis* "did not keep closer, he would fire in upon them and sink them." Entering the Cape Fear River less than a week later, the pirates captured a small boat, which they stripped to use to make repairs to the *Royal James*. The careening operation began, and Stede decided that with the abundance of plundered provisions now onboard the *Royal James*, the pirates would stay in the safety of the Cape Fear River for the next two months. The beginning of October would mark the end of the height of the hurricane season and offer a relatively safe passage south to St. Thomas and Stede's new life as a privateer. Unfortunately for Stede and the crew of the *Royal James*, the first of October would prove a few days too long to linger at Cape Fear.

Back in Charleston, the public clamored for the authorities to take action against piracy. A pirate named Vaughn had appeared at the Charleston bar only a few weeks after Blackbeard's blockade. Following Blackbeard's example, Vaughn had also sent a list of demands into the city. Charleston was once again impotent against the pirate threat and was compelled to deliver the ransom. Governor Johnson wrote to the Lord Proprietors begging for a naval presence, stating, "Hardly a ship goes to sea but falls into hands of pirates."

The outraged citizenry was unwilling to wait months for a response from London and demanded that immediate action be taken. When intelligence reached the city in late August that a pirate ship was careening with two prizes in the Cape Fear River, Charleston's hero and defender Colonel William Rhett proposed to mount an expedition to North Carolina to capture or kill the pirates. Governor Johnson endorsed the plan, and two vessels were pressed into service—the sloop *Henry* with eight cannons, commanded by Captain John Masters and the *Sea Nymph* with eight cannons, captained by Fayrer Hall. The *Henry* was chosen as Rhett's flagship, and with a combined force of 130 men, the two ships sailed from Rhett's wharf on September 10. Sailing across the harbor, both vessels anchored off the western end of Sullivan's Island and took on fresh water and made final preparations. A lookout on the *Henry* spotted a small sloop approaching from the sea that proved to be a trading sloop from Antigua under the command of a Captain Cook. Cook reported to Rhett that he had just been plundered off the Charleston bar by the infamous Charles Vane in a brigantine of twelve guns and 90 men. Vane had been sailing with another pirate named Yeates, and they had also captured

Engraving of Charles Vane from Captain Charles Johnson's *A General History of Pirates.*

a sloop from Barbados, as well as a ship from Guinea that carried over 90 slaves. Once the slaves had been transferred to Yeates's vessel, Yeates apparently had a change of heart about his piratical profession and slipped away from Vane under the cover of night, sailing south with his human cargo. A furious Vane set out in pursuit. Yeates eluded Vane by hiding in the secluded Edisto River. A frustrated Vane returned to the Charleston bar and continued his hunt, intercepting four vessels bound for London, including the *Neptune* and the *Emperor.*

Panic swept through Charleston as news reached the city that the pirate Yeates had landed just south of the city in the Edisto River. However, fear abated when a message was received from Yeates stating that he would deliver his cargo of slaves and surrender himself in exchange for a pardon. Governor Johnson happily agreed.

While they plundered his ship, Cook had heard Vane's crew describing their plan of putting in at a river south of Charleston to careen their brigantine. Rhett immediately gave the order for the *Henry* and the *Sea Nymph* to weigh anchor on September 15 and begin to search for Vane. But Vane's crew had cleverly misinformed Captain Cook about their intentions and had set a course for the Bahamas. Rhett called off the search after a few days and set a course for the Cape Fear River. Faced with a strong northeasterly wind, the voyage to North Carolina was slow, and the two ships did not reach the mouth of the Cape Fear until September 26.

Above the tree line, Rhett could see the mast tops of three vessels less than mile up the Cape Fear River. The channel was notorious for shifting and shoaling, so a pilot was paid to guide the *Henry* and *Sea Nymph* up the river. Bucking the outgoing tide, the channel proved challenging to even the seasoned pilot, and the *Henry* quickly ran aground. Following in the flagship's wake, the *Sea Nymph* also became lodged in the river bottom.

It wasn't long before Stede and the rest of the pirates observed the two motionless masts in the river and believed them to be wayward merchant vessels that would make easy prizes. That night, a group of pirates manned three canoes and paddled downriver with plans to board and plunder the two stranded ships. In the glint of the moonlight, the pirates were chilled to find two heavily armed sloops flying the King's colors. With the rising tide, both the *Henry* and *Sea Nymph* had refloated and now rested at anchor. The canoes quickly scurried back upstream and reported to Stede the ominous threat waiting for them at the mouth of the river.

The pirates and the South Carolinians spent a sleepless night clearing decks and prepping guns for the inevitable fight to come at dawn. The opposing sides could hear the sounds of each other's feverish preparations resonating over the surface of the river. Like a cornered wild beast, Stede became belligerent and unpredictable. He demanded that Captain Manwareing present himself. Stede informed Manwareing that he had no choice but to return all of the prisoners to the *Francis* and *Fortune*. The weary Manwareing had by now been a prisoner onboard the *Royal James* for nearly two months. Manwareing stood by passively as Stede lectured and browbeat him over the treachery and futility of the forces sent against him. Stede had correctly guessed that the two heavily armed sloops waiting for him had been sent from Charleston and he read Manwareing the contents of a letter that he intended to send to Governor Johnson if he escaped. Manwareing would later testify that the contents of Stede's letter threatened "that in case the vessels which then appeared were sent from South Carolina to fight of attack them, and he got clear off...he would burn and destroy all vessels going in or coming out of South Carolina."

Stede knew that some of the crew would be reluctant to take up arms against a force under the authority of the governor of South Carolina. Consequently, he deceived much of the crew into believing that it was none other than Blackbeard waiting for them at the mouth of the river. Stede assured the frightened crew that Blackbeard would surely kill them all if the *Royal James* was captured.

At dawn, Rhett could see the sails being raised on the pirate vessel, and he gave the order for the *Henry* and *Sea Nymph* to weigh anchor. Stede was taking advantage of the ebbing tide to make a run for the open ocean. Outnumbered and outgunned, Stede knew his only hope was to avoid being boarded and engage in a running fight until the *Royal James* could clear the mouth of the Cape Fear River. Rounding a small wooded headland, the *Royal James* came into full view of Rhett. A seasoned mariner, Rhett quickly recognized the pirates' intentions and set the *Henry* on a course to intercept the *Royal James* and block the pirates' escape route to the sea. As the *Henry* bore down, the *Royal James* was forced to maneuver precariously close to the river's western shore. Waiting in reserve, the *Sea Nymph* sailed further downstream in case the pirates were able to outrun the *Henry*.

Stede was just preparing to give the order for the port side cannons to open fire on the *Henry* when he was suddenly and violently thrown forward onto the deck. The *Royal James* had run aground. As the *Henry* drew within a hundred feet, she too grounded on the same shoal. Much further downstream and well out of range, the *Sea Nymph* joined the other two vessels hard aground. The *Henry* and *Royal James* immediately began to exchange small arms fire. Both vessels listed dangerously on their starboard sides, but the pirates had a distinct advantage as the *Royal James*'s deck was inclined away from the *Henry*, and the pirates were able to take cover behind the railing. The deck of the *Henry* was fully exposed to the *Royal James*, and the pirates poured deadly shot into the South Carolinians. The cannons of both ships were essentially neutralized as neither could bring their guns to bear from their tilted decks—the *Henry*'s gunners could not elevate their cannons high enough, and the pirates could not range their cannons low enough.

In between musket volleys, ugly taunts were exchanged by both sides. The pirates lodged insults against King George, and in return, the crew of the *Henry* mocked James III, referring to him as the "Pretender." A contemporary account of the fight that would come to be known as the Battle of the Sand Bars described the action: "The pirates made a wiff in their bloody flag, and beckoned with their hats in derision to our people to come on board them; which they only answered with cheerful Huzza's, and told them it would soon be their turn." Men who dared to poke their heads above the cover of bulwarks were mowed down. Stede noticed Thomas Nichols across the deck, cowering and refusing to fight. Nichols had only recently joined the *Royal James* and had found the pirate life not to his liking. He had refused to sign articles. Nichols would later testify that Stede called to him across the deck and threatened to "blow his brains out" if he did not engage the enemy. Nichols still refused, but as Stede leveled his gun to fire, he was distracted as another pirate was struck and fell dead next to him.

The battle waged for five hours as both ships waited for the next high tide. Regardless of their current advantage, Stede was all too aware that the victor of this battle would be the vessel that refloated first. A great cheer was heard coming from the *Henry* as the battered sloop was the first vessel to ease off the river bottom. The *Sea Nymph* was soon also free, and both vessels began to bear down on the still grounded *Royal James*. His blood still coursing with adrenaline and rage, Stede declared that he would ignite the *Royal James*'s powder magazine and send every man to the river bottom before he would submit to his attackers. Drawing out two pistols, Stede threatened to shoot any man that stood against him. But the rest of the pirates had seen enough bloodshed and decided to take their chances in a courtroom rather than face the certain death of the approaching boarding party. A flag of truce was run up the mast, and the *Royal James* surrendered. The South Carolinians had suffered twelve killed and eighteen wounded in the engagement. Seven pirates were killed and five wounded, two of whom would die later of their wounds.

Rhett remained in the Cape Fear River for three more days while the wounded were tended to and repairs made to the battle-damaged vessels. The *Henry*, *Sea Nymph* and *Royal James*, as well as the pirate prizes *Francis* and *Fortune*, set sail together southbound on September 30, arriving in Charleston on October 3 "to the great joy of the whole province."

North Carolina historical marker at Southport. *Photo by Jennifer Capps.*

# 6

# Judgment

In Charleston, the thirty-six captured pirates were released into the custody of Nathaniel Partridge, the province's provost marshal. There was no formal jail in Charleston, so the crew of the *Royal James* was detained in the Court of Guard building—a small, wooden, two-story structure on the Half Moon Battery. Stede was held separately in Nathaniel Partridge's house at the southeast corner of Tradd and Church Streets. Although some historians have explained Stede's upgrade in lodgings as a result of his status as a gentleman, it was most likely to prevent him from conspiring with his crew before their trial. Stede was soon joined in Partridge's home by the *Royal James*'s boatswain, Ignatius Pell, and then by Stede's friend David Herriot. Both Pell and Herriot had agreed to testify against their fellow pirates in return for immunity. For their protection, the pair was removed from the company of their former crew.

Nathaniel Partridge had a lot in common with the gentleman pirate now in his custody. Partridge was also from the Parish of Christ Church in Barbados, and he may very well have known Stede's father and uncle. Before sailing from Bridgetown in November 1689, Partridge had written a will in which he described his future plans as "bound on a voyage beyond the seas." This "voyage" brought him to Charleston, where he found success and wealth among the large, thriving population of former Barbadians living in the Carolinas. Seven of the earliest governors of the Carolinas had emigrated from Barbados. Partridge had been named provost marshall in 1716 by then governor Robert Daniell. Partridge owned a sprawling plantation, as well as the Charleston home that he now shared with his pirate guests.

The fate of the imprisoned pirates caused Charleston to fall into a state of chaos. Although the pirates had brought terror and insult to the city, there were still, remarkably, many citizens who supported the pirates. Some of the city's merchants had grown rich purchasing and then reselling the pirates' cheap smuggled goods. In addition, many of Charleston's underclass falsely viewed the pirates as seafaring Robin Hoods, preying on the aristocratic and wealthy. Stede became something of a celebrity, particularly in the eyes of many of the women of Charleston. Attorney General Richard Allein noted, "I am sorry to hear some expressions drop from private persons in favour of the pirates, and particularly Bonnet; that he is a Gentleman, a Man of Honor, a Man of Fortune, and one that has had a liberal Educaton." Raucous crowds began to form every night outside of the Court of Guard and Partridge's house. Scuffles would break out between the pirate supporters and those who demanded justice for Stede and his former crew. In response, the General Assembly held an emergency meeting on October 17 at the Parsonage House of St. Phillip's Church, where an act was passed "for the more speedy and regular trial of pirates."

Compounding the city's fragile state came the news on October 21 that the pirate Christopher Moody had returned to the Charleston bar and was preying on vessels. Rumors spread throughout the city that Moody was going to sail into the harbor and rescue his imprisoned pirate brethren. Stede did not believe that Moody would be brazen enough to mount a rescue, but Stede did begin to lay out a plan to escape the city walls and reach Moody. Three days later, disguised as a woman in one of Mrs. Partridge's shawls, Stede, along with David Herriot, slipped through the dark streets and beneath the palisades over Vanderhorst Creek. Waiting for Stede and Herriot was a canoe supplied by Richard Tookerman, one of the city's merchants who had grown rich off smuggled goods. One can only speculate at Herriot's reasoning for fleeing with Stede, since Herriot had only days before turned state's evidence and signed a lengthy deposition describing Stede's crimes since Herriot's capture by Blackbeard at Turneffe. It can only be assumed that the silver-tongued Stede had sold Herriot on the promise of a life of fortune and adventure once they reached Moody. Silently paddled across the harbor by several of Tookerman's slaves, Stede looked back at the walled city fading into the darkness. He could see his *Royal James* riding at anchor near Rhett's wharf. A cold northeasterly wind began to blow, and Stede drew Mrs. Partridge's shawl tightly around his shoulders.

News quickly spread of Stede's escape, and a search began with "hue and cries and expresses by land and by water, throughout the whole province; so that it is hoped he will be retaken." Governor Johnson offered a seven-hundred-pounds-sterling reward for Stede's capture. Although never officially charged with being complicit in the escape, Nathaniel Partridge was fired from his position as provost marshall and replaced by Thomas Conyers. It seemed evident to most that Stede had paid off Partridge or, at the least, had played on the sympathies of his fellow Barbadian to facilitate his escape. Ignatius Pell, who was found still in Partridge's house, later testified that he was tempted to flee with Stede and Herriot but through his "superior virtue" was able to resist temptation.

Determined to move forward with trial, a vice-admiralty court was convened on October 28. Vice admiralty courts were established in the colonies to enforce the Navigation Acts of 1696 and ensure that the Crown received its due revenues from merchant shipping. Crimes of piracy and other maritime felonies fell under the jurisdiction of the vice-admiralty court. The standards and procedures of these courts would seem appalling compared to today's judicial process. The pirates were given no legal counsel and were responsible for their own defense. Arrayed against the pirates were a judge, ten assistant judges, the attorney general and assistant attorney general. The jury of twenty-three all had prior knowledge and prejudices against the pirates. All were from the surrounding province, and some were certainly merchants or planters who had suffered losses at the hands of pirates. There were five eyewitnesses to the pirates' crimes that would testify for the prosecution, including the absent David Herriot; Ignatius Pell; Captain Peter Manwareing, of the *Francis*; Manwareing's first mate, James Killing; and Captain Thomas Read, of the *Fortune*.

The trial was held in the home of shoemaker Garrett Vanvelsin. Vanvelsin would later in his life grow wealthy, achieve the rank of captain in the militia and become involved in insurance, but the decision to use his home as the venue for the trial seems to have more to do with location than with Vanvelsin's promising future. Proprietary records of Charleston show that Vanvelsin and Nathaniel Partridge both lived within the confines of Town Lot Seventy-three at the southeast corner of Tradd and Church Streets. To ensure the safe transfer of Stede back and forth from Partridge's house to trial, Vanvelsin's adjacent house was chosen as the courtroom. Due to the tight confines of Vanvelsin's house and the already large number of judges, prosecutors and jury members, the pirates were tried in groups of five to eight at a time. The pirates were arraigned on two indictments, the first for the seizure and plunder of Captain Manwareing's *Francis* and the second for Captain Read's *Fortune*.

Presiding over the trial was Judge Nicholas Trott. Born in London into a family of drapers and tradespeople, Trott's family had fostered powerful business and marital connections. Through these connections, the precocious Nicholas acquired the position of secretary to the attorney general of Bermuda upon the completion of his legal training at the Inner Temple. In 1703, Trott was appointed chief justice of South Carolina. In this capacity, Trott presided over civil and criminal matters within the province. In one trial of a woman accused of witchcraft, the devoutly religious Trott condemned the defense who denied the existence of witchcraft. Trott said, "We live in an Age of Atheism and Infidelity, and some persons that are no great friends to religion, have made it their Business to decry all stories of apparitions and of witches." In 1716, Trott was promoted to vice-admiralty judge. The Trott name was no stranger to piracy. It was his uncle and namesake, the former governor Nicholas Trott of the Bahamas (often referred to as Nicholas Trott, the elder) who had been bribed by the pirate Henry Avery at Nassau in 1696. Judge Nicholas Trott was an active member of St. Phillip's Church, like his friend William Rhett, and Trott, who was fluent in several languages, spent much of his time translating and explicating the original Hebrew Bible into English. However, also like his friend William Rhett, Trott had his detractors. Many

considered Trott to be a self-righteous bully, and complaints had been made to the governor that Trott had abused his position and authority.

Trott began the proceedings by reading a prepared but compelling charge to the grand jury that defined the vice-admiralty court's authority and power to punish "the heinousness and wickedness of the offense of piracy." He told the grand jury that "the sea was given by God for the use of men, and is subject to Dominion and Property, as well as the Land." His charge outlined the definition and nature of the offense of piracy, quoting both civil and biblical laws.

Judge Nicholas Trott who presided over the trials of Stede Bonnet and his crew.

Not burdened by the rule of impartiality, Trott reminded the jury that "the inhabitants of this Province have of late, to their great cost and damages, felt the evil of piracy, and the mischiefs and insults done by pirates; when lately an infamous pirate had so much assurance as to lie at our bar, in sight of our town, and to seize and rifle several of our ships bound inward and outward." Trott also commended William Rhett and the Charleston citizens that had brought the accused pirates to justice, telling the jury, "We cannot sufficiently commend and honour the zeal and bravery of those persons, who so willingly and readily undertook that expedition against the pirates; and so gallantly acted their parts when they engaged them."

After Trott's impassioned speech, the pirates that stood before the jury must have felt hopeless to conjure any kind of defense. However, when asked for their plea, all thirty-three pirates pleaded not guilty. The pirates had little to offer in the way of defense. When the pirates were asked by Trott if they had anything to say in their defense, most responses were similar to that of the once-impudent Robert Tucker, who stated, "After Captain Thatch [Blackbeard] had taken what we had and left us, Major Bonnet came and told us that he was going to St. Thomas for the Emperor's commission, if there was any to be had. We had but little provisions on board and were forced to do what we have done." Late into the third day of the trial, a moment came that must have brought laughter to the courtroom. After listening to repeated accounts by the pirates of how they had only seized vessels to obtain provisions in order to survive, Trott said, "But pray what did you with so much molasses, which was neither fit to eat or drink?" Both Captain Manwareing and Captain Read gave detailed testimony as to the seizure of their vessels, which was anxiously corroborated by Ignatius Pell, the boatswain of "superior virtue." When the subject of the engagement with Rhett's force in the Cape Fear River was raised, several pirates like Job Bayly said, "We thought it had been a pirate." To which Trott was quick to counter, "But how could you think it was a pirate, when he had King George's colours?" Some provided the same defense as George Dunkin, who insisted that the pirates' actions had been against his will, and he had intended to "leave this course of life." But the prosecution's witnesses were quick to testify that these men were seen receiving their share of the plunder taken out of the *Francis* and *Fortune*.

The court adjourned on November 5. Twenty-nine of the thirty-three pirates were found guilty. Trott read aloud the condemned men's names and said, "You shall go from hence to the place from whence you came, and from thence the place of execution, where you shall be severally hanged by the neck, till you are severally dead."

Among the four men spared was Thomas Nichols, who had narrowly escaped being shot by Stede for refusing to fight against Rhett at Cape Fear. Thomas Gerard, who was a mulatto, was found not guilty when he presented evidence that he had been threatened by Stede to be sold into slavery if he did not sign articles. He further recounted that he did not take any shares of the plunder from the *Francis* or *Fortune*, a claim which was supported by Captain Manwareing. Rowland Sharp and Jonathan Clarke were both able to prove that they were forced men. Clarke had blundered into the company of the pirates in the Cape Fear River and was taken aboard the *Royal James*. When he refused to sign articles, Clarke testified, "He [Stede] said he would make me Governor of the first island he came to; for he would put me ashore, and leave me there." Rowland Sharp related the following harrowing tale, "After I was taken, I went on shore, and traveled four days in the woods without eating or drinking, and could find the way to no plantation, and so was forced to return again, and I refused to sign the Articles; and one of the men came and told me I was to be shot, and I had the liberty to choose the four men that should do it, and the boatswain went about to get hands to beg me off; but I was resolved to make my escape the first opportunity."

While his former crew endured their weeklong trial, Stede was camped across the harbor on the western end of Sullivan's Island. The cold headwind that he had felt in the canoe as he fled from the city proved to be a nor'easter. The storm's strong winds halted Stede, Herriot and their slave companions from traveling any further than the three miles across the harbor to desolate Sullivan's Island. From the beach, Stede could see the large number of anchored merchants ships profiled against the walls of the city. Ship traffic was frozen with the threat of Christopher Moody looming offshore. Turning back toward the ocean, Stede scanned the empty horizon through his spyglass. Herriot chastised Stede, reminding his friend that there had been no sign of Moody in the ten days they had been rotting away on the bug-infested island. Ignoring Herriot's comments, Stede continued his vigil. Moody was his only hope of salvation.

News reached the city of strange smoke coming from the tip of Sullivan's Island. William Rhett guessed correctly that the smoke was coming from the camp of Stede and Herriot. Rhett assembled an armed force and set off across the harbor in a small boat on November 6. Stede, who was still obsessively scanning the horizon for Moody, did not notice Rhett's small boat approaching the back side of the island. Surprising the fugitives, Rhett called for surrender. Someone in Stede's party fired a pistol, and in response, Rhett's men opened fire with their long muskets. David Herriot was struck and fell dead. Two of the slaves were wounded. Stede surrendered for the second time to Rhett and was returned to Charleston. This time, there would be no opportunity for escape, and Stede was placed in the Court of Guard with his former crew. However, the reunion would not last long as the following day, November 8, the twenty-nine condemned pirates were paraded outside the city's southern wall to White Point (today known as the Battery) and hanged. (See Appendix II for complete list of crew hanged November, 1718.)

Riding the wave of Charleston's success against pirates, Governor Johnson resolved to form an expedition to capture Christopher Moody, who was still believed to be lingering off the Charleston coast. Governor Johnson announced that he would be leading this excursion, and four vessels were chosen, including the *Sea Nymph* from the Battle of the Sand Bars, the *Mediterranean*, *King William* and Stede's *Royal James*. The news that the governor would be leading the fleet from onboard the *Mediterranean* roused the spirits of Charleston's citizens, and three hundred men volunteered to join the expedition.

Two suspicious vessels that were suspected to belong to Moody were spotted at the entrance to the harbor. Governor Johnson gave the order for all four vessels to cover their guns and pose as unarmed merchant vessels. As the four vessels sailed out of the harbor, one of the pirate vessels fell for the ruse and hauled the Jolly Roger to its mast top. Sailing between the *Mediterranean* and *King William*, the pirates' call for surrender was met with pummeling broadsides. Both pirate vessels turned and made a run for the open sea. A ferocious battle ensued, which could be seen from the city's ramparts by the Charleston citizenry. After a two-hour running fight, both pirate vessels surrendered. Boarding the decimated pirate ships, Governor Johnson was surprised to find that these ships did not belong to Christopher Moody. The captured vessels were the *New York Revenge* and the *New York Revenge's Revenge* and were under the command of Richard Worley, who had been killed during one of the first broadsides of the engagement.

Moody had received news of the force that Governor Johnson was forming to capture him and had fled south a few days earlier. Worley had unwittingly arrived at the Charleston bar shortly after Moody's departure. Worley's pirate career had lasted only six weeks. He had sailed out of New York in September with eight companions in an open boat.

The small pirate gang met with immediate success and captured two large vessels, which the pirates commandeered for their own use. They soon posed such a threat that the governor of Pennsylvania ordered the royal warship HMS *Phoenix* to sail in pursuit. Worley sailed south to avoid capture by the HMS *Phoenix*, which unfortunately for these pirates, ushered their untimely arrival at Charleston.

His wrists and feet shackled, a dejected Stede sat in the Court of Guard building. He could hear the thunder of cannons coming from the governor's fight with Worley across the harbor. Any hopes that he had of a pirate victory followed by rescue evaporated when he heard the jubilant cheers coming from the crowd on the ramparts of the Half Moon Battery. He knew the pirates had struck their colors and surrendered. Stede was soon joined in the makeshift jail by approximately thirty pirates who had survived the battle. Most of Stede's new cellmates were horribly wounded, and several died of their wounds over the next few days.

On November 10, the vice-admiralty court was again convened at Garrett Vanvelsin's house. Just as with his late crew, Stede was arraigned on two indictments, "for feloniously and piratically taking the sloop *Francis*, with her goods…and the sloop *Fortune*, with her goods." Stede pleaded not guilty to both charges, stating, "My pleading not guilty is because I may have something to offer in my defense; and therefore I hope none of the bench will take it amiss."

Proceeding with the first indictment of the seizure of the *Francis*, the prosecution's star witness, Ignatius Pell, recounted to the jury the now-familiar story of the events leading up to the plunder of Captain Manwareing's vessel. Pell seemed to still have some affection for his former captain. Stede asked Pell, "Don't you believe in your conscience, that when we left Topsail Inlet, it was to go to St. Thomas?" Pell agreed. Judge Trott countered that Stede's former crew had testified "that you [Stede] deceived them; under the pretence of going to St. Thomas." A cool and collected Stede responded, "I am sorry that they should take the opportunity of my absence to accuse me of that that I was free from." Pell aided Stede's defense by painting a picture of Stede as the captain in name alone, pointing to Robert Tucker as the real ringleader. When Trott asked Pell if Stede was the "Commander and Chief among them," Pell replied, "He went by that name, but the Quarter-Master had more power than he." However, regardless of Stede's arguments that he was merely an unwilling participant and the crimes were "contrary to [his] inclination," the fact that he had taken his share of plunder was undeniable. During Captain Manwareing's testimony, Stede asked his former prisoner,

The Nicholas Trott house at 83 Cumberland Street, Charleston. Although its location and positioning next to the Powder Magazine (background) make it unlikely to have been the home of Judge Nicholas Trott, it is still a beautiful example of an eighteenth-century home. The home's current owner, Elise Detterbeck, offers tours. Visit her at www.tourcharlestonbehindthegate.com. *Photo by author.*

"Did you ever hear me order anything out of the sloop?" In an emotionally charged moment in the court room, Manwareing, who also seemed to harbor some fondness for Stede, passionately remarked, "Major Bonnet, I am sorry you should ask me the question; for you know you did which was my all, that I had in the world. So that I do not know but my wife and children are now perishing for want of bread in New England. Had it been only myself, I had not mattered it so much; but my poor family grieves me."

Stede did call one witness for his defense, a young man from North Carolina named James King. King only offered that he had heard second hand that Stede had received a commission from Governor Eden to sail to St. Thomas to receive a privateering license against Spain. An unimpressed Trott said to Stede, "If this be all the evidence you have, I do not see this will be of much use to you." Stede, who had by all accounts remained composed and confident throughout his trial, summarized his defense, eloquently stating:

*May it please you honours, and the rest of the gentlemen, though I must confess myself a sinner, and the greatest of sinners, yet I am not guilty of what I am charged with. As for what the boatswain says, relating to several vessels, I am altogether free; for I never gave my consent to any such actions for I often told them, if they did not leave off committing such robberies, I would leave the sloop; and desired them to put me on shore. And as for Capt. Manwareing, I assure your honours it was contrary to my inclination. And when I cleared my vessel at North Carolina, it was for St. Thomas and I had no other end or design in view but to go there for a commission. But when we came to sea, and saw a vessel, the quartermaster, and some of the rest, held a consultation to take it but I opposed it, and told them again I would leave the sloop, and let them go where they pleased. For as the young man said...that I had my clearance for St. Thomas.*

The jury was unmoved, and their foreman, Timothy Bellamy, stood and read the jury's verdict—guilty. The court reconvened the next day to try Stede for the second indictment for the seizure of Captain Read's *Fortune*, but a despondent Stede retracted his previous plea and reentered a plea of guilty. The following day, Nicholas Trott read a long statement berating Stede for his crimes. The pious Trott reminded Stede that "being a gentleman that have had the advantage of a liberal education and being generally esteemed a man of letters, I believe it will be needless for me to explain to you the nature of repentance and faith in Christ, they being so fully and so often mentioned in the Scriptures, that you cannot but know them." Trott explained that the court's punishment paled in comparison to God's punishment for murderers, quoting Revelations, "for murderers have their part in the lake which burneth with fire and brimstone, which is the second death." But Trott did offer Stede the consolation "so that if now you will sincerely turn to [Jesus], though late, even at the eleventh hour, he will receive you." Trott then pronounced his sentence: "That you, the said Stede Bonnet, shall go from hence to the place from whence you came, and from thence to the place of execution, where you shall be hanged by the neck till you are dead. And the God of infinite mercy be merciful to your soul."

# 7

# The End of a Golden Age

The busy vice-admiralty court was hurriedly convened again on November 19. Members of Worley's crew were dying of their wounds at an alarming rate at their jail inside the Court of Guard. Governor Johnson was anxious to try and then summarily execute the remaining pirates before they could succumb to their wounds. Nicholas Trott presided over the weeklong trial that adjourned on November 24. Nineteen pirates were found guilty and sentenced to hang.

Stede watched horrified as the nineteen pirates were forcibly removed from the Court of Guard and loaded into a wagon to make the trip to White Point. Some were so badly injured that they had to be propped up underneath the scaffolding as the noose was looped around their necks. With the execution of Worley's crew, Charleston had hanged forty-eight pirates in the space of just three weeks. Five hundred miles away in the once-called "pirate utopia" of Nassau, nine other pirates were preparing to be hanged on the ramparts of the fort overlooking Nassau harbor.

The rumors that Stede and Blackbeard had heard in Nassau the previous spring of a new governor being sent to Nassau to hang those who would not accept the royal pardon had proven to be true. Woodes Rogers arrived in Nassau in late July 1718. Rogers had led a remarkable life, including a more than three year privateering voyage that resulted in the circumnavigation of the globe. Before being appointed governor of the Bahamas, Rogers had been most famous for his rescue of Alexander Selkirk from the island of Juan Fernandez, three hundred miles off the coast of Chile. Selkirk would become the inspiration for Daniel Defoe's *Robinson Crusoe*.

The beautiful and popular Battery at the tip of the Charleston peninsula was, in the early eighteenth century, a swampy area called White Point. Located outside the city walls, White Point was where condemned pirates were hung and buried. *Photo by author*.

Many of Nassau's pirates, including Blackbeard's former mentor, Benjamin Hornigold, accepted the royal pardon that Rogers brought from London. Hornigold further received a commission from Rogers to hunt pirates, and he set off in search of Charles Vane in September 1718. Unable to find Vane, who was preying on vessels off Charleston at the time, Hornigold did capture a group of pirates who now awaited execution on the ramparts of the fort at Nassau. On December 12, just as the command was about to be given to haul away the barrels that supported the condemned, Rogers stepped forward and pardoned one of the pirates. For the remaining eight pirates, "the stage fell, and the prisoners were suspended." Although eight men paled in comparison to the multitude hanged in Charleston the previous month, the execution sent a strong and clear message that pirates were no longer welcomed in Nassau. Through Rogers's efforts, the Bahamas's national motto became "Pirates expelled, commerce restored."

Stede had taken up the pen in a last effort to save his life. Writing a series of pitiful letters that were published in the Charleston newspapers, Stede garnered sympathy by playing on the heartstrings of the city. In one particularly lamenting letter to Governor Johnson, Stede wrote:

Woodes Rogers, governor of the Bahamas. The walls of the fort overlooking Nassau harbor can be seen behind Rogers. The globe next to Rogers represents his circumnavigation during his privateering voyage from 1708 to 1711.

*I Have presumed on the Confidence of your eminent Goodness to throw myself, after this manner at your Feet, to implore you'll be graciously pleased to look upon me with tender Bowels of Pity and Compassion; and believe me to be the most miserable Man this Day breathing; That the Tears proceeding from my most sorrowful Soul may soften your Heart, and incline you to consider my Dismal State, wholly, I must confess, unprepared to receive so soon the dreadful Execution you have been pleased to appoint me; and therefore beseech you to think me an Object of your Mercy.* (See Stede's entire letter to Governor Johnson in Appendix III)

Stede's letters had a lasting effect on many of the ladies of Charleston, but the women were not alone in their compassion for Stede. Stede's former captor, William Rhett, offered to raise funds and personally escort Stede to London "so that his case might be referred to his majesty." However, Governor Johnson was unmoved. After several stays of execution, December 10 was firmly fixed as Stede's appointment with the gallows.

When dawn broke the morning of December 10, Stede knew there would be no more delays, no more stays and no more chances at escape. No angry mob would be coming to his rescue. His appeals for mercy had fallen on deaf ears. Stede had played his last card, and judgment day had come. He hadn't slept all night in anticipation of the horrifying, choreographed events that would occur in Charleston that day. Through the window of the Court of Guard on Half Moon Battery, he could see the calm morning waters of the harbor and the open sea beyond. Just over the walls of the Half Moon Battery lay trackless miles of sea where he could sail away and remember the last two years of his life as only a bad dream. But Bonnet's journey today would be a short one. It would be the same journey that twenty-nine of his former crew and nineteen of Richard Worley's men had made weeks before.

His hands were bound in front of him as he was defiantly removed from the Court of Guard and hoisted into a horse-drawn cart. Down the length of Broad Street, Stede could see the throngs of people lining the street all the way to Charleston's western gate. Whatever composure and fortitude Stede had displayed during his trial had now abandoned him. Gone were the silken shirts and cravats of the gentleman "man of letters." The dirty,

Colonel William Rhett's grave at St. Phillip's Church in Charleston. Rhett died in 1722. In a strange twist, Nicholas Trott married William Rhett's widow, Sarah, in 1727. Both Nicholas Trott and Sarah lie buried in unmarked graves next to William Rhett. *Photo by author.*

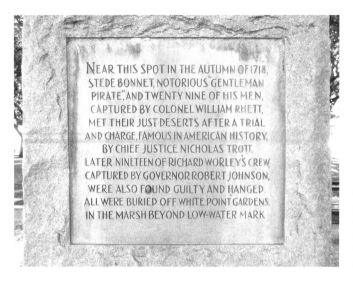

NEAR THIS SPOT IN THE AUTUMN OF 1718,
STEDE BONNET, NOTORIOUS "GENTLEMAN
PIRATE", AND TWENTY NINE OF HIS MEN,
CAPTURED BY COLONEL WILLIAM RHETT,
MET THEIR JUST DESERTS AFTER A TRIAL
AND CHARGE, FAMOUS IN AMERICAN HISTORY,
BY CHIEF JUSTICE NICHOLAS TROTT.
LATER NINETEEN OF RICHARD WORLEY'S CREW,
CAPTURED BY GOVERNOR ROBERT JOHNSON,
WERE ALSO FOUND GUILTY AND HANGED.
ALL WERE BURIED OFF WHITE POINT GARDENS,
IN THE MARSH BEYOND LOW-WATER MARK

The pirate monument at the Battery in Charleston, South Carolina. *Photo by author.*

worn, quivering figure in the cart that the crowd now observed must have made for a pitiful sight. The hanging of a pirate was grand theater in the eighteenth century, and all of Charleston's citizens turned out to watch the spectacle. A mixture of words of support and insults came from the crowd. If he were lucky, a supporter would have handed some rum up to the cart to help dull his senses before he reached the gallows. The city's gate was opened, and the crowd followed the cart along the outer wall to the marshy area called White Point. Crossing the bridge over Vanderhorst Creek, Stede got his first glimpse of the noose hanging from the crossbeam of the simple, square-framed wooden gallows.

Stede's execution was timed to coincide with the low tide. In accordance with Admiralty law, pirates were buried in shallow, unmarked graves in the mud just "beyond the low water mark." Stede's spirit would find no peace as his remains would shift in the mud as the movement of the tides eternally washed over his grave. No headstone or marker could be placed on Stede's grave, so no mourners could visit or lay flowers.

The cart was positioned beneath the wooden frame, and the noose tightened around Stede's neck. Before him, Stede saw his shallow grave dug in the pluff mud. A representative of the Admiralty stood at the foot of the gallows carrying a silver oar—the symbol of the Admiralty. Someone had pushed a bouquet of posies into Stede's manacled hands as the preacher began his prayer for the dying. The condemned was offered the opportunity to address the crowd, but the usually eloquent Stede was now described as "scarce sensible," and he was unable to form any words.

A nod from the Admiralty official would be the signal for Stede to be pushed from the cart into space. The fall from the cart would not be enough to break his neck. Stede's fate would be a slow suffocation as he twitched and struggled. Some of his supporters would rush forward and pull on his legs to expedite the process and end his misery.

One can only speculate as to the last thoughts that raced through Stede's panicked mind as he stood beneath the gallows. He may have thought of Blackbeard's treachery. Stede certainly had to feel that Blackbeard's actions had set into motion the events that now brought him to the noose. He must have thought that the grave dug before him should be for Blackbeard. However, unknown to Stede and the rest of Charleston was the fact that Blackbeard had been dead for nearly three weeks.

Much like Stede, Blackbeard had returned to piracy shortly after receiving his pardon from Governor Eden in Bath. In September, while Stede was holed up in the Cape Fear River, Blackbeard and Charles Vane were hosting a pirate party on Ocracoke Island. News reached lieutenant governor Alexander Spotswood in Virginia of the party, and Spotswood became convinced that Blackbeard was turning Ocracoke into a base for pirate operations, like Nassau. At this time, Spotswood was facing harsh criticism in Virginia. He was spending huge amounts of the tax money on a homebuilding project in Williamsburg, which the citizens mockingly called the "Governor's Palace." Anxious to divert attention from his "palace" and garner some good press, Spotswood met with Captain Brand onboard the HMS *Lyme* to lay out a plan to capture or kill Blackbeard.

Alexander Spotswood's Governor's Palace in Williamsburg, Virginia. *Photo by author.*

Jean Leon Gerome Ferris's *The Capture of the Pirate, Blackbeard* depicts the battle between Blackbeard and Lieutenant Robert Maynard onboard the deck of the *Jane* at Ocracoke Inlet.

Two sloops, the *Ranger* and the *Jane*, left the Chesapeake Bay and sailed for Ocracoke Inlet under the command of Lieutenant Robert Maynard. On November 22, the two sloops spotted the *Adventure* riding at anchor at Ocracoke. Blackbeard, on the *Adventure*, called out, "Damn you for villains, who are you? And whence you came?" Maynard, onboard the

*Jane*, answered, "You may see by our colors we are no pirates." Raising a mug of rum, Blackbeard bellowed, "Damnation seize my soul if I give you quarter or take any from you!" Pressing the pursuit of the *Adventure*, both the *Ranger* and *Jane* ran aground. Blackbeard fired a devastating broadside into both vessels. Maynard ordered the surviving crew to retreat below deck into the hold of the *Jane*. When the smoke cleared, Blackbeard saw the deck of the *Jane* nearly empty except for the dead and wounded. Grappling hooks were thrown from the *Adventure*, and Blackbeard ordered his pirates to storm onboard the *Jane* and kill any survivors. As the pirates rushed the *Jane*'s deck, Maynard sprung his trap and signaled his hidden crew to burst from the hold up the companionway. A confused hand-to-hand battle ensued in the tight confines of the *Jane*'s deck. The pirates were outnumbered but still fought with ferocity. In an epic moment of the battle, Blackbeard and Maynard faced off against one another. Maynard fired a shot into Blackbeard's hulking body, which did not seem to slow the pirate down. Blackbeard swung his huge cutlass at Maynard, breaking the lieutenant's saber at the hilt. Maynard fell to the deck, and Blackbeard strode forward to deliver the final blow. As Blackbeard raised his sword over his head, a Scottish sailor approached from behind and buried his sword into Blackbeard's neck. The mighty Blackbeard collapsed to the deck. With a second blow, Blackbeard's head was severed from his body.

A post-battle autopsy found Blackbeard's body to have no less than five pistol shots and twenty severe cuts. Blackbeard's head was hung from the bowsprit of the *Adventure*, and the gruesome trophy was delivered to Alexander Spotswood back in Virginia. The most infamous pirate in history had truly died a pirate's death.

Back on the gallows in Charleston, perhaps Stede's last thoughts were more serene. His thoughts may have drifted to his family and life back in Barbados. It had only been just over a year and a half since he sailed out of

Blackbeard's severed head was hung from the bowsprit and returned to Alexander Spotswood in Virginia.

Engraving of Stede Bonnet hanged in Charleston, December 10, 1718.

Carlisle Bay, but his former life as a Barbadian planter seemed like a lifetime ago. The image of the small stone that marked the grave of Allamby in St. Michael's churchyard may have entered his mind. The devastating loss of his firstborn had set into motion a pirate's life that now led him to death on the gallows in Charleston.

He felt the sudden pressure of a hand on his back, and Stede Bonnet, the gentleman pirate, stepped into eternity.

# By The King, A Proclamation, For Suppressing Pyrates

Whereas we have received Information, that several Persons, Subjects of Great Britain, have since the twenty-fourth day of June, in the Year of our Lord 1715, committed divers Pyracies and Robberies upon the High-Seas, in the West Indies, or adjoining to our Plantations, which hath and may Occasion great Damage to the Merchants of Great Britain, and others trading into those Parts; and tho' we have appointed such a Force as we judge sufficient for suppressing the said Pyrates, yet the more effectually to put an End to the same, we have thought fit, by and with the Advice of our Privy Council, to Issue this our Royal Proclamation; and we do hereby promise, and declare, that in Case any of the said Pyrates, shall on or before the fifth of September, in the Year of our Lord 1718, surrender him or themselves, to one of our Principal Secretaries of State in Great Britain or Ireland, or to any Governor or Deputy Governor or any of our Plantations beyond the Seas; every such Pyrate and Pyrates so surrendering him, or themselves, as aforesaid, shall have our gracious Pardon, of and for such, his or their Pyracy, or Pyracies, by him or them committed before the fifth of January next ensuing. And we do hereby strictly charge and command all our Admirals, Captains, and other Officers at Sea, and all our Governors and Commanders of any Fort, Castles, or other Places in our Plantations, and all other our Officers Civil and Military, to seize and take such of the Pyrates, who shall refuse or neglect to surrender themselves accordingly. And we do hereby further declare, that in Case any Person or Persons, on, or after, the sixth Day of September 1718, shall discover or seize or cause or procure to be discovered or seized, any one or more of the said Pyrates, so refusing or neglecting to surrender themselves as aforesaid, so as they may be brought to Justice, and convicted of the said Offence, such Person or Persons, so making such Discovery or Seizure, or causing or procuring such Discovery or Seizure to be made, shall have and receive as a Reward for the same, viz. for every Commander of any private Ship or Vessel, the Sum of £100 sterling for every Lieutenant, Master, Boatswain, Carpenter, & Gunner, the Sum of £40 for every inferior Officer, the Sum of £30 for every private Man, the Sum of £20. And If any Person or Persons, belonging to and being Part of the Crew of any such Pyrate Ship or Vessel shall on or after the said sixth Day of September, 1718, seize and deliver, or cause to be seized or delivered, any Commander or Commanders, of such Pyrate Ship or Vessel, so as that he or they be brought to Justice, and convicted of the said Offence, such Person or Persons, as a Reward for the same, shall receive for every such Commander, the Sum of two hundred pounds sterling which said Sums, the Lord Treasurer, or the Commissioners of our Treasury for the Time being, are hereby required, and desired to pay accordingly.

Given at our Court, at Hampton-Court, the fifth Day of September 1717, in the fourth Year of Our Reign.

George R.
God save the KING.

# Crew of Stede Bonnet Hanged at White Point, November 1718

Robert Tucker of Jamaica
Edward Robinson of Newcastle upon Tyne
Neal Paterson of Aberdeen
William Scott of Aberdeen
William Eddy, alias Neddy, of Aberdeen
Alexander Annand of Jamaica
George Rose of Glasgow
George Dunkin of Glasgow
John Ridge of London
Matthew King of Jamaica
Daniel Perry of Guernsey
Henry Virgin of Bristol
James Robbins, alias Rattle, of London
James Mullet, alias Millet, of London
Thomas Price of Bristol
James Wilson of Dublin
John Lopez of Oporto, Portugal
Zachariah Long of Holland
Job Bayly of London
John-William Smith of Charleston
Thomas Carman of Maidstone in Kent
John Thomas of Jamaica
William Morrison of Jamaica

# Appendix II

Samuel Booth of Charleston
William Hewet of Jamaica
John Levit of North Carolina
William Livers, alias Evis
John Brierly, alias Timberhead, of Bath Town, North Carolina
Robert Boyd of Bath Town, North Carolina

*Appendix III*

# Stede Bonnet's Letter to Governor Johnson, November 1718

Honoured Sir;

I Have presumed on the Confidence of your eminent Goodness to throw myself, after this manner at your Feet, to implore you'll be graciously pleased to look upon me with tender Bowels of Pity and Compassion; and believe me to be the most miserable Man this Day breathing; That the Tears proceeding from my most sorrowful Soul may soften your Heart, and incline you to consider my Dismal State, wholly, I must confess, unprepared to receive so soon the dreadful Execution you have been pleased to appoint me; and therefore beseech you to think me an Object of your Mercy.

For God's Sake, good Sir, let the Oaths of three Christian Men weigh something with you, who are ready to depose, when you please to allow them the Liberty, the Compulsion I lay under in committing those Acts for which I am doom'd to die.

I entreat you not to let me fall a Sacrifice to the Envy and ungodly Rage of some few Men, who, not being yet satisfied with Blood, feign to believe, that I had the Happiness of a longer Life in this World, I should still employ it in a wicked Manner, which to remove that, and all other Doubts with your Honour, I heartily beseech you'll permit me to live, and I'll voluntarily put it ever out of my Power by separating all my Limbs from my Body, only reserving the use of my Tongue to call continually on, and pray to the Lord, my God, and mourn all my Days in Sackcloth and Ashes to work out confident Hopes of my Salvation, at that great and dreadful Day when all righteous Souls shall receive their just rewards:

And to render your Honour a further Assurance of my being incapable to prejudice any of my Fellow-Christians, if I was so wickedly bent, I humbly beg you will, (as a Punishment of my Sins for my poor Soul's Sake) indent me as a menial Servant to your Honour and this Government during my Life, and send me up to the farthest inland Garrison or settlement in the Country, or in any other ways you'll be pleased to dispose of me; and likewise that you'll receive the Willingness of my Friends to be bound for my good Behavior and Constant attendance to your Commands.

I once more beg for the Lord's Sake, dear Sir, that as you are a Christian, you will be as Charitable as to have Mercy and Compassion on my miserable Soul, but too newly awaked from an Habit of Sin to entertain so Confident Hopes and Assurances of its being received into the arms of Blessed Jesus, as is necessary to reconcile me to so speedy a Death; wherefore as my Life, Blood, Reputation of my family and future happy State lies entirely at your Disposal, I implore you to consider me with a Christian and Charitable Heart, and determine mercifully of me that I may ever acknowledge and esteem you next to God, my Saviour, and oblige me ever to pray that our heavenly Father will also forgive your Trespasses.

Now the God of Peace, that brought again from the Dead our Lord Jesus, that great Shepherd of the Sheep thru' the Blood of the everlasting Covenant, make you Perfect in every good work to do his Will, working in you that which is well pleasing in his Sight thro' Jesus Christ, to whom be Glory forever and ever, is the hearty Prayer of Your Honour's

Most miserable, and, Afflicted Servant,
Stede Bonnet

# Selected Bibliography

Alleyne, Warren. "A Barbadian Pirate." *Bajan* (June–August, 1973).

Bates, Susan Baldwin and Harriot Cheves LeLand, eds. *Proprietary Records of South Carolina, Volume III*. Charleston, SC: The History Press, 2007.

*Boston News-Letter*. 1719.

*British Public Records Office*. available in South Carolina Room, Charleston County Library Main Branch. Charleston, SC.

Brock, R.A., ed. *Official Letters of Alexander Spotswood*. Richmond, VA, 1885.

Butler, Lindley. *Pirates, Privateers and Rebel Raiders of the Carolina Coast*. Chapel Hill, NC: University of North Carolina Press, 2000.

Coker, P.C. *Charleston's Maritime Heritage, 1670–1865*. Charleston, SC: CokerCraft Press, 1987.

Cordingly, David. *Pirate Hunter of the Caribbean, The Adventurous Life of Captain Woodes Rogers*. New York: Random House, 2011.

————. *Under The Black Flag: The Romance and the Reality of Life Among the Pirates*. New York: Harcourt Brace and Company, 1995.

Duffus, Kevin P. *The Last Days of Black Beard the Pirate*. Raleigh, NC: Looking Glass Productions, 2008.

Earle, Peter. *The Pirates Wars*. New York: St. Martin's Press, 2003.

Ellms, Charles. *The Pirates' Own Book*. Philadelphia, PA, 1837.

Hogue, Lynn L. "Nicholas Trott: Man of Law and Letters." *South Carolina Historical Magazine* (1973).

Hughson, Shirley Carter. *The Carolina Pirates and Colonial Commerce, 1670-1740*. Baltimore, MD: The Johns Hopkins Press, 1894.

Johnson, Captain Charles. *A General History of the Robberies and Murders of the Most Notorious Pirates*. New York: First Lyons Press, 1998.

Konstam, Angus. *Blackbeard: America's Most Notorious Pirate*. Hoboken, New Jersey: Wiley and Sons, 2006.

Lee, Robert E. *Blackbeard The Pirate: A Reappraisal of His Life and Times*. Winston-Salem, NC: John F. Blair, 1974.

Leland, John G. *Stede Bonnet: Gentleman Pirate of the Carolina Coast*. Charleston, SC: Charleston Reproductions, 1972.

Lewis, Jon E., ed. *The Mammoth Book of Pirates*. Philadelphia, PA: Running Press, 2007.

Little, Benerson. *The Sea Rover's Practice: Pirate Tactics and Techniques, 1630-1730*. Dulles, VA: Potomac Books, Inc., 2007.

McIntosh, William. *Indians' Revenge: Including a History of the Yemassee Indian War*. Charleston, SC: Booksurge Publishing, 2009.

———. "Stede Bonnet's Trial." Charleston, SC. unpublished paper.

Morgan, Kenneth O. *The Oxford History of Britain*. New York: Oxford University Press, Inc., 2010.

Porcher, Jennie Rose and Anna Wells Rutledge. *The Silver of St. Phillip's Church, 1670–1970*. Charleston, SC: St. Phillip's Church, 1970.

Rediker, Marcus. *Between the Devil and the Deep Blue Sea: Merchant Seamen, Pirates and the Anglo-American Maritime World, 1700-1750*. Cambridge, UK: Cambridge University Press, 1987.

Salley, A.S., ed. *Register of St. Phillip's Parish, 1720–1758*. Columbia: University of South Carolina Press, 1971.

Schomette, Donald G. *Pirates on the Chesapeake*. Centreville, MD: Tidewater Publishers, 1985.

South Carolina Department of Archives and History. 8301 Parklane Road, Columbia, SC.

Stevenson, Robert Louis. *Treasure Island*. London: Cassell and Company, 1883.

Strangward, Ethel Partridge. *Nathaniel Partridge of Charles Town, South Carolina and His Descendants*. DeLeon Springs, FL: E.O. Painter Printing, Company, 1985.

*The Tryals of Major Stede Bonnet and Other Pirates*. London: Rose and Crown in St. Paul's Church Yard, 1719.

Williams, Lloyd Hanes. *Pirates of Colonial Virginia*. Richmond, VA: The Dietz Press, 1937.

Woodard, Colin. *The Republic of Pirates*. Orlando, FL: Harcourt, Inc, 2007.

# About the Author

C hristopher Byrd Downey (Captain Byrd) received his degree in history from Virginia Tech. He has worked in the maritime industry for over fifteen years. He lives in Charleston, South Carolina. A United States Coast Guard licensed captain, Captain Byrd offers pirate boat tours of Charleston Harbor. Visit him at www.captainbyrds.com.

*Photo by Tina Mckelvaney.*

Visit us at
www.historypress.net